A Student's Guide
to Corneille

STUDENT GUIDES TO EUROPEAN LITERATURE

General Editor: Brian Masters

Molière, by Brian Masters

Sartre, by Brian Masters

Goethe, by F. J. Lamport

Rabelais, by Brian Masters

Corneille, by J. H. Broome

Böll, by Enid Macpherson

Racine, by P. F. Butler

Camus, by Brian Masters

Kafka, by Anthony Thorlby

Gide, by Christopher Bettinson

Brecht, by Michael Morley

Horváth, by Ian Huish

Thomas Mann, by Martin Swales

A Student's Guide to Corneille
Four Tragedies

by

J. H. BROOME

Professor of French
University of Keele

HEINEMANN EDUCATIONAL BOOKS
LONDON

Heinemann Educational Books Ltd
22 Bedford Square, London WC1B 3HH
LONDON EDINBURGH MELBOURNE AUCKLAND
HONG KONG SINGAPORE KUALA LUMPUR NEW DELHI
IBADAN NAIROBI JOHANNESBURG KINGSTON
EXETER (NH) PORT OF SPAIN

ISBN 0 435 37575 X

Set, printed and bound in Great Britain by
Fakenham Press Limited, Fakenham, Norfolk

Contents

Author's Note

Where the commentaries in the following pages are directly concerned with the texts of Corneille's plays, names of characters are normally given in the French form used by him, e.g. 'Chimène', 'Auguste'. Elsewhere, as in discussions of source material or historical background, the original Spanish or Latin forms (e.g. 'Ximena', 'Augustus') are used where they seem more appropriate, or more in keeping with English usage.

Foreword

Like other volumes in the series, this book is a supplement to, and not a substitute for, first-hand acquaintance with original texts, and is written to meet the practical needs of students, including those in the upper forms of schools, where Corneille is often read for the first, and sometimes for the last, time.

Although he shares with others the advantages and disadvantages attaching to the status of 'prescribed author', the appreciation of his plays may be impeded by a number of special difficulties. For example, he is almost always the earliest author encountered in the first stages of the study of French literature, with the result that an obstacle of historical remoteness is added to what may still be a serious language-barrier. He is also an intrinsically difficult writer because of the density and intellectual sophistication of his texts. Furthermore, the ostensibly 'heroic' atmosphere of his best-known productions, combined with the literary and dramatic conventions of the seventeenth century, may create an impression that they are museum-pieces rather than living works – an impression sometimes strengthened by comparison with his younger contemporary Racine, whose tragedies seem to be more approachable and more in line with modern sensibilities. Finally, although Corneille wrote thirty-two plays, only about a fifth of his very varied output can really be said to have survived, even in France, despite the efforts of critics to rehabilitate the rest. Consequently, few people are ever in a position to survey his work as a whole; and those who do are far from agreement as to its general significance, if indeed it has one.

In view of these difficulties, it would be quite unrealistic to try to cover the whole of Corneille in a short introduction; so general discussion is here confined to the introductory chapter, which provides a brief historical background, and to the conclusion, which raises some of the major problems of criticism. Otherwise, attention is directed to the four tragedies which, rightly or wrongly, still constitute his main claim to fame and which readers are most likely to encounter in practice. These are analysed in some detail, not for the sake of mere narration, but in order to approach him from the inside and show him first and foremost as a practical playwright and craftsman.

Over the years, interpretation of his work has been heavily influenced by changing fashions in criticism and philosophy; but while this is inevitable and even desirable, it is doubtful whether a balanced appraisal of his intentions can ever be arrived at without close consideration of his development and transformation of source-material. In the following pages, as much attention as possible is paid to this aspect of the subject, as a prerequisite for critical discussion.

1

Introduction

The Career of Corneille

Pierre Corneille was born at Rouen on 6 June 1606. As the son
of an advocate, he belonged to a class of provincial bourgeois
with a strong instinct for social advancement, which was to be
confirmed in his own life. Of his childhood little is known that
could bear upon his literary career, but in adolescence he was a
distinguished pupil of the Jesuits. Although his education was
in no way exceptional, it is important for two main reasons:
first, because it provided a solid basis of classical learning,
particularly in Latin; and secondly, because his outlook was
probably affected to some extent by the theology and moral
philosophy of his teachers, which would tend to emphasize the
importance of freewill, and hence of human effort, in the
processes of salvation. Although some of his commentators
have sought to minimize the importance of religious influences
on his work, Corneille appears to have remained personally
committed to the general principles of his Christian upbringing;
and the allegedly 'heroic' characteristics of his writings are at
least compatible with the particular doctrines to which he was
exposed.

After leaving college he studied law and was received as an
advocate at Rouen in 1624. On the strength of this, his father
purchased for him in 1628 a dual appointment in the provincial
administration (as *Avocat du Roi au siège des Eaux et Forêts ...
et à l'Amirauté de France*); and some insight into his character
may be gained from the fact that despite his success as a dramatist, he carried out his functions conscientiously for twenty-two

years. Although he was not a practising advocate in the ordinary way, critics have always sensed in his plays a flavour of the law, and of forensic oratory.

Corneille responded to the call of literature at an early age. By 1625 he was writing verse, and in 1629 his first play, a comedy entitled *Mélite*, was performed successfully at the Marais theatre in Paris. This was followed by a tragi-comedy, *Clitandre* (1630–31) and, over the next three years, by four other comedies: *La Veuve*, *La Galerie du Palais*, *La Suivante* and *La Place Royale*. They are not great plays, nor even 'comic' plays in the same sense as the masterpieces of Molière later in the century, but they are by no means negligible. They demonstrate Corneille's lively interest in contemporary manners, and display skills which he was to apply later in the field of tragedy, such as the ability to create and control complex situations, and analyse with considerable finesse moral problems and human relationships. Although based on realistic observation, the plots of some of them evolve in an atmosphere of illusion, deception and inconstancy which marks them as products of the preclassical or 'Baroque' phase of French literature. It also creates an interesting background for the serious works to follow, which it is possible to interpret as commentaries on man's urge to master and rationalize the vicissitudes of an uncertain existence.

These early exercises in dramatic composition were completed by two contrasting works which suggest that Corneille was still seeking his way and had not quite found a formula for outstanding success. In 1635 he produced his first tragedy, *Médée*, inspired by Seneca, and presenting a version of the famous story in which the heroine, after her betrayal by Jason, destroys her own children. Though weakened by a failure really to come to terms with a supernatural element in the subject-matter, this work is noteworthy for the portrayal of Medea who, as a 'criminal' heroine, displays already the force, energy and self-assertion associated with his best-known characters. With *Médée*, Corneille had found the right kind of character, but not, as yet, the right kind of story for the particular bent of his genius; and it is perhaps a sign of frustration that he turned away from tragedy to write *L'Illusion Comique* (1635–6), a theatrical experiment based on the idea of a play-within-a-play. This is a pure Baroque entertainment which, after long neglect, has attracted much interest in recent years for technical reasons, and exemplifies admirably its author's versatility. It too contains a character – the braggart Matamore – offering certain points of comparison with Corneille's serious heroes.

The production of *Le Cid* in 1637 marks the beginning of the most impressive period in his career, during which he set the standards for French neo-classical tragedy. This epoch-making play, of Spanish inspiration, stirred up a great critical controversy which ended by strengthening Corneille's confidence in his own powers. It was followed by the 'Roman' tragedies *Horace* (1640) and *Cinna* (1640–41); by the brilliant religious play *Polyeucte* (1642–3); by the less distinguished but still admirable *Mort de Pompée* (1643–4) and *Rodogune* (1644–5); and by the excellent situation-comedy of *Le Menteur* (1643–4), based, like *Le Cid*, on a Spanish model. This, together with a sequel, *La Suite du Menteur* (1644–5), shows again Corneille's flexibility; but plays written during the next few years reveal a falling-off, if not in his technical powers, at least in his ability to pick inspiring subjects. With *Nicomède* (1651), which pushes a 'heroic' formula to a logical but not very dramatic conclusion, he seemed to be losing touch with public taste; and this was confirmed in 1652 when the play *Pertharite* proved a total failure, despite a genuinely interesting political content, and the exploitation of a dramatic situation not unlike that in *Andromaque* which, fifteen years later, was to win acclaim for his young rival Racine.

After the disaster of *Pertharite* Corneille turned away from the theatre, and for some years found an outlet for his poetic gifts in a verse-translation of Thomas à Kempis's *Imitation of*

Christ; but in 1659 he returned to drama with a new treatment of a traditional subject in *Œdipe*. From 1659 to 1674 he produced in all ten plays and some important theoretical discussion, notably in three *Discours sur le poème dramatique* (1660); and two years before his death in 1684 he rounded off a distinguished record with a revised and complete edition of his plays. The last series of plays made comparatively little impression on a new generation which had become increasingly indifferent to political subjects and heroic overtones, and correspondingly responsive to Racine's tragedies of passion. Consequently, Corneille may be said to have outlived his public; and this is reflected in the attitude of subsequent generations, who have tended on the whole to see his later works as evidence of a steady decline. Loss of popularity does not, however, necessarily imply loss of skill, and recent criticism has corrected this impression to some extent, and accorded to them, as to the early comedies, an increased measure of esteem. They are in fact varied in tone and subject and almost always competent, if not brilliant; and his very last play *Suréna* (which makes concessions to changing taste and, indeed, to 'Racinian' style) will bear comparison with anything written after the period of his greatest triumphs.

In spite of these revaluations, however, it remains true that his greatest contribution to the development of the French theatre, and of the *tragédie classique* in particular, was made between 1636 and 1643. To set his achievement in perspective, it is useful to recall briefly the fortunes of the theatre in the previous period, and certain aspects of dramatic theory which influenced his work.

The Theatre Before Corneille

Although neo-classical tragedy is associated above all with the seventeenth century, it is the outcome of processes and aspirations going back to the Renaissance. At the beginning of the sixteenth century, such drama as existed in France was mainly a survival of medieval traditions in the form of farces and mystery-plays; but these traditions were clearly moribund. The possibility of a serious renewal of drama arose, however, with the emergence in the middle of the century of the group of writers known as the *Pléiade*, the greatest of whom were the poets Ronsard and Joachim du Bellay. In 1549 Du Bellay wrote a famous manifesto entitled *La Défence et illustration de la langue française*, expressing contempt for the old tradition and preaching, as the way of salvation for French literature in general, the imitation of the writings of classical antiquity. In the field of drama, this doctrine was put into practice by another member of the group, Etienne Jodelle, whose play *Cléopâtre Captive* (performed 1552–3, published 1574) is customarily regarded as the first significant achievement in the process of renewal. Throughout the second half of the century a considerable quantity of literary drama was produced, with a wide variety of themes and subject-matter drawn from pagan antiquity, Biblical stories and historical events, including the religious wars. Later, at the turn of the century, the popularity of macabre and romanesque subjects was a manifestation of baroque taste.

Apart from tragedy and some imitative essays in literary comedy, notably by Pierre Larivey, the sixteenth century also experimented with new or intermediate genres such as the pastoral and the tragi-comedy, a good example of which is *Bradamante*, produced in 1582 by Robert Garnier, perhaps the best dramatist of his time. As its name implies, this hybrid form of drama normally works out a serious plot to a happy ending, and it maintained its popularity long enough to tempt Corneille himself. One of its leading practitioners was Alexandre Hardy (1570–1631), a mediocre but prolific author whose work during the first decades of the seventeenth century makes him a dominating figure in the French theatre before the emergence of Corneille.

Hardy's importance derives partly from the fact that he was much more of an actor's playwright than his predecessors, who had been essentially men of letters. Though not without literary skill, his main assets were responsiveness to public taste and a feeling for box-office considerations; and he furnished material directly to the actors of the Hôtel de Bourgogne, a permanent theatre which had long remained a stronghold of medieval tradition. His career represents, therefore, a compromise between literary aspirations and the needs of a living theatre; and although his work remained highly irregular, he could at least extract genuine dramatic actions from old stories. Moreover, by suppressing certain traditional features such as the use of the chorus, he created some of the conditions necessary for the emergence of the highly-concentrated neo-classical drama. What was still needed, however, was a clarification of purpose in terms of dramatic theory; and it must be borne in mind that most of Corneille's works were written against a constant background of theorizing.

Dramatic Theories

Corneille's acknowledged masterpieces are written in accordance (more or less) with rules and conventions, the best-known of which are of course the 'three unities' of action, time and place, commonly believed – not quite correctly – to have been enunciated in the *Poetics* of Aristotle. Although the latter does provide a basis for the idea of a single action taking place in a single day, he was less concerned to hand down precepts than to comment on the practices of Greek dramatists. Nevertheless, the *Poetics* must be regarded as the fountain-head of most of the theorizing, starting from the proposition that the aim of art in general is imitation. In discussing degrees of elevation in the objects of imitation, Aristotle arrives at a distinction between comedy and tragedy, but his detailed views on the former have not survived. Of his observations on tragedy, the most important for the seventeenth century are those concerned with content rather than form, and particularly with plot and character.

For him, the real basis of unity is provided not by a specific character, but by the action itself, which he conceives as a 'whole', visible as such, of adequate magnitude and complete in itself. In other words, as a philosopher engaged in a process of rationalization, Aristotle sees a plot as constituting ideally a logical sequence; and anything that is merely episodic and not strictly relevant is frowned upon. The way of attaining this dramatic unity is through observance of universal truth rather than historical particularities (since the function of the poet is not the same as that of the historian). According to Aristotelian principles, therefore, a good tragic plot would be a strictly organized chain of causes and effects, consisting typically of a 'tragic error' entailing reversal of fortune, a series of incidents and complications, and a final discovery or recognition of the truth in some catastrophic denouement. The immediate object of this action would be to excite certain emotional responses, specified as pity and fear, and to do this mainly through fundamental ironies of situation involving people who, preferably, should not be positively hostile or indifferent to each other. And since Aristotle's thinking is conditioned to some extent by religious ritual, the ultimate effect on the spectators is supposed to be therapeutic, as some kind of emotional purgation or *katharsis*.

Reduced to these simple terms, Aristotle's theory of a tragic action has a plausible appearance, but is in fact full of ambiguities and obscurities; and the same can be said of the conception of a tragic hero or protagonist, which is the other very influential element in the *Poetics*. Here, the main points are that the character should be 'good', appropriate or true to type, true to reality (where this is applicable), and consistent (or at least 'consistently inconsistent'). There is, however, a qualification of the first and rather obscure point, in that Aristotle claims that the character should not be wholly faultless nor wholly bad, since these extremes might produce the wrong emotional responses.

Apart from the ideas of Aristotle (with which Corneille is by no means wholly satisfied), a major source of doctrine is the so-called *Ars Poetica* of Horace, which contains about thirty precepts, some trivial, but others very important in the seventeenth century. For example, Horace encourages the view that traditional subjects are safest for the aspiring author; and argues that poems should be homogeneous – a point which leads towards 'unity of tone' and hence the tendency to reject any mingling of tragic and comic. He also preaches extreme care in the selection of episodes; discourages the representation of violence; counsels the avoidance of divine interventions as much as possible, in the interests of ordinary human credibility and verisimilitude; and emphasizes the moral or didactic aim of art.

Between them, Aristotle and Horace provide food for thought on most of the important aspects of poetic drama, including plot, characterization, moral content, the unities and other formal matters; but their observations are supplemented by contributions from many other sources, ranging from the fourth-century writer Donatus to the host of commentators thrown up by the Renaissance. Consequently, the theories being fought over in France during the youth of Corneille are not simply compounds of Aristotle and Horace, but doctrines which have already been commented on, amended, inflated and distorted by generations of critics, of whom some of the most influential are sixteenth-century Italians such as Vida and Castelvetro. Not surprisingly, therefore, the arguments stirred up around *Le Cid* by hypersensitive rivals like Chapelain and Scudéry have an air of pedantry about them.

Corneille and Dramatic Theory

Corneille's position in this respect is somewhat ambiguous. He claims to have begun writing plays in blissful ignorance of any rules, but the preface to *Clitandre* in 1632 includes a reference to Horace. On the other hand, it is doubtful whether he studied Aristotle seriously until the 'Querelle du *Cid*'. Thereafter, his work does appear increasingly regular; but his willingness to conform is rarely based on anything but practical utility, and his own theoretical discussions usually contain independent lines of thought.

For example, he obviously accepts in principle the Aristotelian view that a dramatic action should have its own inner logic and unity; and his plots show evidence – even to excess – of careful intellectual organization. But he does not necessarily follow thereafter the simple patterns that can be deduced from the *Poetics*, and it would be surprising if he did, in view of the complexities of moral analysis which were fashionable in his day. Similarly, although he goes part of the way with Aristotle in matters of characterization, some of his figures, such as the martyr, Polyeucte, or the criminal queen, Cléopâtre, in his play *Rodogune*, convey the impression of having been created specifically to challenge or test the validity of the norm of 'middling virtue'. Again, though he would obviously agree that pity and fear are emotions proper to tragedy, the response of 'admiration' also enters into his calculations. Despite variations in public estimates of what is admirable, this is a particularly interesting point; first because it is, conceivably, his way of trying to make sense of Aristotle's much-debated theory of *katharsis*, and secondly because it is one of the reasons why the quality of *générosité* enters so prominently into his characterizations. Whatever else they may be, his best-known figures are *généreux* – a term which, while it may sometimes have connotations of outgoing liberality such as are associated with the English 'generous', is really much nearer to the 'patrician' sense of the Latin *gens* from which it is derived, and implies respect for certain ideals or standards established in the family or group. In short, his characters have *style* – a thoroughbred quality capable of transcending the sum of actions which may not, in fact, be admirable in themselves, at least from a moral standpoint. Such *générosité* in the characters is an important manifestation of Corneille's individuality; and, as a final example of his independent outlook, it is worth noting that he tends to stand apart from contemporary opinion in the matter of truth and probability. Whereas it is generally felt, through the joint influence of the ancient theorists, that probability is more conducive to the suspension of disbelief, and hence to emotional involvement, than extraordinary facts, Corneille has a marked tendency to explore the backwaters of history for the kind of exceptional truth which is stranger than most fictions. In this, as in other things, he seems to be testing rather than following received opinion; and it is this streak of unorthodoxy, rather than the conventional aspects of his work, which helps to explain why he is still *le grand Corneille*, and why the plays discussed in the following pages are among the finest in the repertory of the French theatre.

2
Le Cid

The Subject

It is somewhat ironic that the play which did so much to establish the pattern for neo-classical tragedy in France should be based on subject-matter which, theoretically, would be more in keeping with Romantic taste. It derives from medieval Spain, 'Cid' being the name or title bestowed on a typical 'hero' of those times, i.e. a figure distinguished mainly by military exploits which subsequently, by normal processes of folklore, took on epic proportions and left him as representative, in the public imagination, not only of physical prowess, but of all the moral and even religious virtues. The original of this figure is Rodrigo (Ruy) Diaz de Bivar, born during the eleventh century near Burgos, who was for a time *Alferez* or Constable of Castille, but is known to have served Moorish leaders as well as Christian kings. He married Ximena, daughter of the Count of Oviedo, and shortly before his death in 1099, was engaged in a project to drive the Moors out of Spain altogether. This, combined with his success on the occasions when he was actually fighting them, accounts for the transformation of his character in stories and epics of the twelfth and thirteenth centuries, and his ultimate appearance as the complete hero of chivalry in the *Romancero del Cid*, part of a seventeenth-century collection of stories in epic or ballad form.

This is one of Corneille's acknowledged minor sources, together with a *History of Spain* by the Jesuit writer Juan Mariana; but the major inspiration for *Le Cid* is a Spanish play by Guillen de Castro: *Las Mocedades del Cid* (The Youthful

Exploits of the Cid), first printed in 1618. It is particularly important not because it transferred the subject from epic to dramatic literature, but because its author realized that such a transfer could not be made without a process of artistic selection, and concentration upon some specific episode or feature within a great saga. One such feature, capable of acting as a focus of interest, was presented by the marriage of the hero; because during the transmission of the legends it became accepted that Rodrigo's wife, Ximena, was the daughter of a man whom he had killed in a duel. In its simplest form (as it appears, for example, in the *Romance Primero* quoted by Corneille) this circumstance is curious but not particularly dramatic, in so far as Ximena is said to have been orphaned as a mere child, and to have asked the king to marry her to Rodrigo years afterwards, in accordance with a medieval principle of *justice*, so that he might replace the lost father. Later, however, the idea of *love* crept into the tradition, bringing with it, of course, a possibility of conflicting loyalties; and one reflection of this appears in the *History* of Mariana which, in a passage also mentioned by Corneille, describes Ximena as being much attracted by Rodrigo's qualities, and asking the king either to marry them or to punish the young man according to the law. In this version, the conception of justice has changed and there is love (and possibly blackmail!) at least on Ximena's side, before the *marriage*. But although this is a major development in the story, it is still de Castro who must be credited with having divined its full potential and introduced the idea of mutual love before the *duel*, although in his rendering their love is not known to Rodrigo's father.

Las Mocedades del Cid is, therefore, by far the most important of the sources, because in it the death of Ximena's father, the Count, becomes the *obstacle* to marriage. Corneille never concealed his debt to de Castro; but this does not mean that he had nothing to do but imitate the Spanish play, for *Le Cid* is in every sense a new artistic creation, adapted to the tastes and ethics of a different nation at a particular time in its cultural evolution. The nature of his formal achievement can hardly be appreciated without a brief examination of de Castro's play, which is divided into three 'days' or acts, and presents events occurring over about three years and in eight places (allowed for in staging by the use of a multiple décor). In outline, *Las Mocedades del Cid* develops as follows.

ACT I

At Burgos, Rodrigo is knighted before the Court, including the Infanta Urraca and Ximena, who are both in love with him.

In the royal palace, Ximena's father, the Count of Gormas, slaps the face of Rodrigo's father Don Diego, when the king names him governor of the young prince Sancho in preference to the Count, who, unlike Diego, is still in his prime.

At his home, Don Diego, in his desire for vengeance, tries in vain to brandish the sword of his ancestors; and then tests the strength and spirit of his three sons. He bites the finger of Rodrigo, the eldest, and when the latter flies into a rage, nominates him to fight the Count in defence of the family honour, unaware of his love for Ximena. Despite his natural reluctance, Rodrigo accepts his unpleasant duty and, in front of the palace, provokes and kills the Count, in the presence of the Infanta, Ximena and Don Diego. He then escapes with the help of the Infanta.

ACT II

Ximena, displaying her handkerchief stained with her father's blood, demands justice of the king: Diego defends his son's action, and the king defers his decision.

Rodrigo appears before Ximena, in her house; and begs her to do her duty and kill him. She admits that she does not hate him, but insists that she must demand his punishment.

The scene then changes to the countryside, and a series of

episodes occur, showing Rodrigo's emergence as a hero by a great victory over Moorish invaders, at the head of five hundred of his father's adherents. He returns to the palace with his prisoners, and the king grants him the title of Cid ('lord') first used by one of the captive leaders.

But Ximena again appears, demanding justice and accusing him of unknightly conduct; and reluctantly the king banishes Rodrigo.

ACT III

More than a year later, the Infanta is shown, bent on subduing and renouncing her love for Rodrigo because of her rank – and to the advantage of Ximena. But Ximena comes to demand justice for the third time. She is deceived into thinking that he is dead, and reveals her grief; but on learning the truth, refuses to admit that she loves him, and promises to give herself to whatever champion shall avenge her and bring her Rodrigo's head. There is then a mystical episode in which Rodrigo gives help to a leper, who, transformed into St Lazarus, blesses him and prophesies his future glory. Thereafter Rodrigo fights the giant Don Martin Gonzalez, champion of Aragon – and of Ximena; and having defeated him sends a messenger to announce to Ximena the arrival of a knight from Aragon bearing Rodrigo's head. Deceived again into thinking him dead, Ximena confesses her love and begs the king to allow her to escape a hateful marriage by going into a convent.

But then Rodrigo appears, leaves at the door the head of Gonzalez on a pike, and, bearing his own head on his shoulders, claims the right to marry Ximena unless she will sever it herself. The king and the court urge her to accept this interpretation of the conditions of the combat, and the marriage is arranged forthwith.

Such is de Castro's adaptation of the legendary material: a work which, despite its irregularity and grotesque elements, is at least held together by themes of a sort, relating to the conflict of love and honour and the contrast between public glory and private frustrations. It also has potentially sympathetic characters; is based on strong situations; combines agreeably the pathetic and the heroic, and brings together the familiar and the exotic. It has, in fact, most of the ingredients which, in more recent times, have gone into many a swashbuckling epic of the screen; and if, as seems likely, Corneille was first attracted simply by its potential entertainment-value, there would be no reason to quarrel with this. It also, however, offers a fruitful subject for experiment to anyone interested in the prospects for a 'regular' theatre of an elevated kind; and it would not be unfair to Corneille to suggest that in the production of his first masterpiece, refinement of this rough-hewn material plays almost as great a part as invention.

Corneille's Adaptation of the Subject

The first and obvious refinement consists in pruning away certain specific features of the Spanish source. These are: (i) all episodes which merely maintain the epic atmosphere in a quantitative rather than a qualitative sense; (ii) any direct representation of physical violence (except for the famous *soufflet*); (iii) visible effects of violence, such as the bloodstained handkerchief; (iv) anything so grotesque as to offend 'reason' as well as sensibility – e.g. the head on the pike; (v) anything of a mystical nature – e.g. the episode of the leper; (vi) anything which impairs excessively the serious tone (e.g. a burlesque episode of a cowardly shepherd narrating in a partly humorous way the victory over the Moors). To compensate for some of these omissions, Corneille adds one episode: a second encounter of the lovers, which creates a climax of the moral action.

The second major refinement is the concentration or redistribution of the remaining material in such a way as to conform as far as possible with the unities of time, place and action. In this, Corneille's success is only partial, as he admitted. It is notorious, for example, that the events which he retains could scarcely take place within twenty-four hours, especially the appearance and defeat of the Moors; though he has done his best to meet this problem in the interests of credibility by transferring the main setting of the play from Burgos to Seville. This, however, involves an anachronism, since Seville was in Moorish hands at the relevant period. Similarly, even with this amendment, the events cannot take place credibly in one precise location; and the first performances were staged with a modified form of multiple set, allowing for up to three locations in a given act. And finally, Corneille can be charged with a technical infringement of the unity of action, in that he retains the figure of the Infanta and allows her to go through her private drama of love and renunciation of Rodrigo without integrating this very satisfactorily with the main action. Consequently, although the role of the Infanta provides an additional source of pathos, strengthens the theme of self-possession and the claims of love and duty, and enhances the status of Rodrigo by her love, purists are apt to argue that her effect upon events is not sufficient to justify her retention, or that Corneille has not made the most of her.

On balance, therefore, it may be said that in *Le Cid* he has observed the spirit rather than the strictest letter of the 'rules'; but in an *Avertissement* of 1648 he takes his stand, very sensibly, on the assertion that the work conforms to Aristotelian principles not by observing conventions which that philosopher did not in fact formulate as a system, but in the character and situation of the hero: a noble man involved in unmerited hardship and persecuted by his own lover.

Having purged the subject of what he considers its worst excrescences and brought it into line with the tastes of a more enlightened public, Corneille is left with a hard core of external or physical events, in the form of the three major 'perils' which provide the main substance of the three 'days' conceived by de

Castro: two duels with a battle in between them. These must be retained if only by report, as required by the conventions; but the suppression of the grotesque events surrounding the second duel has led to the invention of the character of Don Sanche, a rival of Rodrigo who replaces Gonzalez as Ximena's champion. This done, Corneille now has a free hand to adapt his material to a five-act structure, the interest of which will derive not from the physical events but from the psychological processes which surround, produce or result from them.

The Dramatic Mechanism

Preparation for, and reaction to the first 'peril' provide the material for Acts I and II, in which a lively pace is set almost from the beginning. Act I is not merely expository but highly dramatic in that it illustrates from different angles a major reversal of fortune, as the lovers' high hopes of marriage are dashed by the quarrel of their fathers, which occurs in the third of the six scenes. The first two of them heighten the effect of this disaster by a delicate analysis of the sentiments of the two women who will be affected by it: Chimène and the Infanta; and the succeeding ones depict in brilliant succession the anguish of the aged Don Diègue, his demand that his son should defend his honour, and the even deeper anguish of Rodrigue, whose inner debate and final acceptance of his tragic obligation to fight Chimène's father rounds off the act with the famous *stances*. These, though lyrical in form, are among the most dramatic of soliloquies.

Act II is centred on the duel itself; and while this cannot be staged, the absence of the spectacle is more than compensated for by the tension which Corneille has created around it. First there is a momentary *détente* as the Count debates the possibility of repudiating his own hasty act, only to reject it through pride; then, in Scene 2, there is a kind of prefiguring of the duel as Rodrigue, an untried fighter, challenges the older man. This preserves for the audience the actual emotions connected with the duel itself; and while the outcome is awaited, Corneille has created an opportunity to exploit suspense in a further analysis of the hopes and fears of Chimène and the Infanta, the alternations of which are prolonged by the simple device of reporting the duel in two stages. But even as the first 'peril' of Rodrigue is culminating in his unseen victory over the Count, the second one is being prepared by a report to the king, in Scene 6, that the vessels of Moorish invaders have been sighted. Thus, the announcement in Scene 7 that Rodrigue has killed his adversary comes to the king at a moment when he himself has decided that the Count has merited punishment, yet sees himself in need of the Count's military talents. Consequently it is in a situation where private concerns are becoming inseparable from public issues that Chimène comes to the king to demand for the first time the punishment of Rodrigue; and Don Diègue comes to plead for his son and offer himself as a sacrifice, if atonement be deemed necessary. In these circumstances, there can be no hasty judgement, and the situation remains open pending the deliberations of a council, on which the king proposes to base his decision.

In the course of Act III no outstanding physical action occurs; and Corneille has reserved it for one of the climaxes of the moral action, in the form of the meeting between Rodrigue and the lover whose father he has just killed. This encounter, criticized by some of Corneille's contemporaries on grounds of taste, is based directly on the source, and provides one of the noblest and most pathetic centre-pieces in the whole of his theatre.

It is prepared by three short scenes which, amongst other things, introduce Rodrigue's rival Don Sanche, who offers his services as Chimène's champion, so announcing and rationalizing to some extent the third 'peril' of Rodrigue. Chimène, however, sees this offer only as a last resort, preferring – ostensibly – to wait upon the king's justice; and her feelings are made clear in Scene 3, the immediate prelude to the moving encounter, rising to a kind of 'duet', in which the couple declare their undying love and mutual respect, even though fulfilment now seems impossible because of the claims of family honour, which Rodrigue has met, and Chimène must pursue in seeking his death. This scene attains a lyrical beauty which Corneille rarely achieves in his later plays; but so far as the private drama of the lovers is concerned it represents an impasse which can only be broken from the outside. The break comes, however, in the last two scenes of the act, as Don Diègue impresses on Rodrigue that the threat of the Moorish invaders is the occasion either for death (which Rodrigue claims to seek) or for a glory which may change his situation in relation to the king's justice.

It is therefore in the interval between Acts III and IV of this re-structured play that Rodrigue's second 'peril' is deemed to arise; and so the whole of Act IV can be devoted to the reactions of the court to a great victory which does indeed transform the fortunes of Rodrigue in so far as it makes him a public hero. The first two scenes concentrate on Chimène, and the Infanta's efforts to persuade her to abandon her claim for justice; and Scene 3 contains Rodrigue's celebrated *récit* or narration of his victory, one of the classic examples of this literary substitute for action, the outcome of which is that the king is now unwilling to punish him. But amidst the public rejoicing and admiration, Chimène comes again to raise the private issue and demand justice; and this is the occasion (as in the Spanish play) for the king to trap her into betraying her true feelings by telling her that Rodrigue is dead. But although, by half-fainting, she does betray them, she still presses her claim for justice and the punishment of Rodrigue; and so persistent is she in her dedication to principle that the king yields, at least to the extent of permitting a further duel between Rodrigue and *one* champion, and subject to the proviso that she shall marry the winner. Technically, this is an evasion of royal responsibility and a gamble on probabilities, with the reflection, presumably, that if

Chimène's champion dies, this can be construed as the punishment of folly. So, the third 'peril' can now arise, as Don Sanche repeats his previous offer to fight on Chimène's behalf; and preparations for and reactions to it can form the substance of a final act designed to prolong as much as possible the reversals of fortune.

It begins strongly with the only episode actually invented by Corneille, i.e. a second encounter of the lovers and another climax of the moral action, in which Rodrigue, by stating his intention to let himself be killed, virtually forces Chimène to beg him to fight seriously and save her from marriage to Don Sanche. Not surprisingly, the result of this charming blackmail (which seems to be a reversal of an element in one of the sources) leaves Rodrigue in a mood to fight the entire Spanish nation, if need be, and psychologically prepared to face his second duel. While the outcome of this is awaited, Corneille takes the opportunity to dispose of the episodic figure of the Infanta, who is now shown renouncing her love for Rodrigue. This causes a regrettable drop in tension; but it picks up again in Scene 4, with Chimène still obstinately refusing to abandon publicly the principle of her struggle against Rodrigue. In fact, it requires a misunderstanding to weaken her as, in Scene 5, the sight of Don Sanche returning with his sword leads her to think that he has defeated Rodrigue, whereas he has been defeated, and spared by his opponent. It is a premature explosion of anger and grief which brings her at last to confess her love in the presence of the king and Don Diègue, and to make possible the happy ending suggested by history. Corneille here uses a device of comedy; but it is, of course, a more acceptable substitute for the grotesque denouement of de Castro. The play is left open, with the suggestion of a year's delay before marriage, and the idea that in the meantime the further glory of Rodrigue may overcome the last resistance of Chimène's scruples. So, the play breaks off, not with certainty, but with the restoration of the *hopes* for the fulfilment of a love which has been beset with tribulations, as Chimène sensed that it would be, at the very beginning.

Corneille's recasting of his subject is certainly not flawless, as critics were quick to point out; but comparison of this version with that of de Castro shows clearly why *Le Cid* has a special place in the history of the French theatre. In place of a picturesque but undisciplined spectacle, it offers psychological drama with a solid core of moral problems; and it creates at least the illusion of transforming a collection of episodes into a strictly-organized chain of causes-and-effects ('illusion' in the sense that the vital turning-point provided by the arrival of the Moors remains fortuitous). Moreover, the merits of organization are matched by the general quality of the verse in which it is written; for, despite occasional forced expressions and obscurities, Corneille has taken full advantage of the lyrical, rhetorical and dramatic potentialities of the Alexandrine. But if *Le Cid* has remained the most popular of his works, this is because in refining the material he has also managed to preserve a certain indefinable atmosphere of youthful ardour and adventure. It has, indeed, so often been considered a play for the young at heart that it is easy to underrate its seriousness, and to overlook features which point the way to the more austere works which were to follow it. But it is above all in its themes, developed with great intellectual rigour, that *Le Cid* exemplifies what will be most typical and complex in his contribution to the theatre.

The Themes

Its complexity may be indicated, paradoxically, by what seems to be its most straightforward characteristic: namely, the heroic quality. Of all Corneille's works, *Le Cid* is perhaps the one which could be considered heroic by definition, if only because of the status of Rodrigue in the background of Spanish tradition. But Corneille is not particularly concerned with the latter's public exploits, except in so far as they are related to the private drama; and it can be argued that what he is really interested in is *Chimène*. This could, no doubt, be explained by the increasing influence of women upon literary taste when the play was written; but a simpler explanation is that in the source-material, the most intriguing circumstance is, after all, that the lady married her father's killer, apparently with general approval. So long as this event is conceived in terms of an orphaned child and a primitive justice requiring a father-substitute, no great problem arises. But as soon as it is presented in terms of adult relationships and ethics, in a society dominated by a code of honour, the marriage itself becomes the most 'heroic' aspect of the subject, especially from the woman's point of view; because it involves the overcoming of an obstacle of such magnitude as to make it seem an act 'contre nature'. In short, the marriage not only poses psychological problems, but must raise, in the long run, philosophical problems, particularly of an ethical nature; and it is in the exploration of such matters, as well as in its formal qualities, that *Le Cid* is the first of a line of master-pieces.

One curious feature of the work, as compared with its immediate successors, is that this exceptional action or culmination of events lies outside the play itself, ostensibly because there is an issue of decorum or *bienséance* which requires a decent interval to elapse, and is thus incompatible with strict observance of the unity of time. But it is obvious that except for the early events producing the first duel, and consequently the obstacle to marriage, the play as a whole is orientated to this historical or legendary conclusion. And the problems which interest Corneille are: by what stages it could happen; whether the power of love would suffice by itself to bring it about; whether other reasons would have to be invoked; and whether or to what extent circumstances would have to change. The sources provide some, but not all of the answers; and it is in Corneille's further probings that a number of leading themes arise, the first of which concerns the nature of love itself.

Theoretically, a woman might marry the killer of her father
for several reasons, including overwhelming desire or passion,
but so far as Corneille is concerned, this would seem to be ruled
out both by the code of honour and the tastes of the audience
for whom he is writing. The alternative is a conception of love
as containing enough positive moral value to outweigh, or at
least to balance, the moral objections to marriage in this
particular situation. This is, in fact, the concept of love – i.e.
'amour-estime' – which prevails in *Le Cid*; and it has a number
of origins in courtly literature, Stoic philosophy and so on. And
it involves not only the idea of love being directed to the most
worthy object, but the obligation of lovers to prove themselves
worthy of love. It means, therefore, that the conflict in the
minds of the lovers is not simply between 'love and duty',
but between two forms of duty; and it produces the paradox that although Rodrigue may provoke Chimène's hatred
if he does his duty and fights the Count, he will also forfeit
her esteem – and therefore her love – if he does *not* do his
duty.

> Je dois à ma maîtresse aussi bien qu'à mon père:
> J'attire en me vengeant sa haine et sa colère;
> J'attire ses mépris en ne me vengeant pas.   (vv. 322–4)

Similarly, Chimène is in duty bound to demand Rodrigue's
death; and would forfeit *his* love if she did not demand it.

> Tu t'es, en m'offensant, montré digne de moi;
> Je me dois, par ta mort, montrer digne de toi. (vv. 931–2)

It is this reciprocity – a kind of contract – which keeps the
strange events within the field of morality; and the other aspect
of the paradox is, of course, that the more the lovers combat
each other, the more their love is enhanced. So, given this
conception of love in the first place, there is no question of it

being completely destroyed, even by the death of the Count. Equally, though, there is, provisionally, no question of its fulfilment, but rather, the possibility of Rodrigue's death. But if he is *not* punished, the moral enhancement of their love through suffering would at least provide *one* of the conditions necessary for the justification of a hypothetical marriage. Putting it another way, the nature and growth of their love through mutual respect does not make marriage possible: it makes it not morally impossible. But the relationship is at an impasse unless other circumstances change; and one possibility of change is still the death of Rodrigue.

It is at this point, however, that circumstances do change, and that *political* themes come into play; for the duel which has led to the Count's death is not only a private offence against Chimène, but is also a political offence in that it deprives the state of its greatest defender, as Chimène points out.

> D'un jeune audacieux punissez l'insolence:
> Il a de votre sceptre abattu le soutien,
> Il a tué mon père.   (vv. 650–52)

Since this has happened at a moment of danger to the state, the king might well punish Rodrigue; but as we know, the arrival of the Moors creates a new situation in which Rodrigue himself becomes a public hero. This introduces the theme of the *raison d'état* (which will recur in other plays of Corneille); and, faced with the choice between punishing the private offence and pardoning the saviour of the state, the king does not hesitate long before bowing to the claims of political expediency. Henceforward, he will do nothing for Chimène except try to *console* her; and we are left with the proposition that justice is not absolute, but relative. It is this proposition which the Infanta tries to urge upon Chimène.

> Ce qui fut juste alors ne l'est plus aujourd'hui (v.1175)

Thus, by a combination of force (his own physical prowess, which will be displayed again in the second duel) and political reasons, Rodrigue survives the threat to his existence posed by Chimène's duty – and another condition is fulfilled for a hypothetical marriage. And one of the most interesting aspects of this development is that it shows Corneille (following de Castro) working a variation on the original material, for whereas in the primitive form of the story Rodrigue replaces the Count in his *private* capacity as protector of Chimène, he now replaces the Count in a *public* capacity as defender of the state. This does not, of course, solve Chimène's moral problem; but in the play it ensures positive public sympathy for the lovers, which is yet another condition that has to be met if the marriage is to be rendered plausible.

Nevertheless, public sympathy cannot operate in the void; and at the point where Rodrigue becomes a hero, the public (i.e. the king and the court) does not know whether Chimène still loves him, let alone whether she would marry him. So, three more stages have to be passed in this movement towards the marriage: namely, the public *revelation* of her love; then (a very different thing), her public *admission* of it; and finally, a public admission in the presence of Rodrigue himself. The first of these is provided for by her involuntary reaction to the king's deliberate pretence that Rodrigue has been killed in battle; and the second by her own misunderstanding of the outcome of the second duel, which she has herself brought about, and her voluntary avowal of love, in the mistaken belief that it may lead her to refuge in a convent. This is the essential step, from the *public* point of view, as Don Diègue seems to be saying:

> Enfin elle aime, sire, et ne croit plus un crime
> D'avouer par sa bouche un amour légitime. (vv. 1741–2)

These movements, it should be noted, are based not on reason but on emotion, or what the Infanta calls elsewhere 'la surprise des sens' (v. 98); and the avowal is made not with a view to marriage, but in the belief that it is impossible. It is only when the king has *commanded* her to marry Rodrigue (thus taking over the function of the father who would have 'commanded' her to love him, had circumstances been different) that she can make a further declaration – and even then it is negative rather than positive in form:

Rodrigue a des vertus que je ne puis haïr.   (v. 1803)

This cautious acceptance of a 'command' to marry may, of course, be taken as prim and maidenly delicacy, and is certainly so regarded by the king, who assures her that in a year's time the *point d'honneur* which is still troubling her will have ceased to do so, and been outweighed by the public glory accruing to Rodrigue in the meantime. So, Corneille can bring down the curtain on this story of 'perfect love', having exploited a number of themes and convergent circumstances to provide a *probability* of marriage which will, no doubt, send the audience away with some degree of assurance that things have a way of working out for the best in the end.

But Corneille does not actually show this happening; he merely uses in a more skilful and effective way the time-scale of the third part of de Castro's version, and leaves it to the audience to decide, not whether a marriage will take place (since 'history' guarantees that it will), but whether a *happy* marriage is conceivable in view of what has occurred. If the answer is yes, *Le Cid* is a *tragi-comedy*, but if not, it is a *tragedy* – and opinions have varied about this. The question is not purely academic, either, because after being labelled *tragi-comédie* from 1637 to 1643, the work was thereafter styled a *tragédie*. This suggests that the nominal happy ending is a theatrical device, and not necessarily the conclusion to be reached by extrapolating from the *themes* of the play. There may be no firm answer to this problem, but special attention should be paid to the final speeches, especially that made to the king by Chimène, on whom, notwithstanding his command, the onus of moral decision still rests.

> Relève-toi, Rodrigue. Il faut l'avouer, sire,
> Je vous en ai trop dit pour m'en pouvoir dédire.
> Rodrigue a des vertus que je ne puis haïr;
> Et quand un roi commande, on lui doit obéir.
> Mais à quoi que déjà vous m'ayez condamnée,
> Pourrez-vous à vos yeux souffrir cet hyménée?
> Et quand de mon devoir vous voulez cet effort,
> Toute votre justice en est-elle d'accord?
> Si Rodrigue à l'Etat devient si nécessaire,
> De ce qu'il fait pour vous dois-je être le salaire
> Et me livrer moi-même au reproche éternel
> D'avoir trempé mes mains dans le sang paternel?
>
> (vv. 1801–12)

Although Chimène admits that she cannot hate Rodrigue's qualities, and accepts the principle of obedience to the king, it is to be noted that most of the speech is interrogative (the last part of it being, indeed, a modification of an original version expressing categorically her resistance). According to this last utterance, she is, at the end of the play, no more convinced of the propriety of the marriage, from a moral standpoint, than she was in the earlier stages; and is still reluctant to incur a *reproche éternel* by her own volition.

The king's answer is that *time* and circumstance will legitimize the marriage and overcome *eternal* morality (as it has legitimized Rodrigue's previous action); and that the private *gloire* of Chimène will somehow be safeguarded and guaranteed by the public reputation of the Cid, as though an additional *quantity* of achievements on the plane of politics and power could outweigh the *quality* of moral principle. This is, to say the least, a dubious proposition, even from a king; and it is not an answer to Chimène's assertion that, technically, she is to be married to Rodrigue as a reward for his services to the state, and will still be in some sense an accessory after the fact of her father's death.

We are left, therefore, with the 'historical' fact of marriage, but no clear idea of the final mental attitudes of the parties concerned, and hence of its status. If they are not happy, it will be because Chimène, in particular, will have been unable to overcome the scruples of reason which she is proclaiming in her last speech. But if they are happy, it will be because of something 'above' reason – i.e. the redemptive and elevating power of love; or something 'below' reason – i.e. the compromising of moral principle through the force of habit and social pressures; or perhaps a combination of both. There is a problem here to which, philosophically speaking, there is no simple, rational answer; and Corneille has not tried to provide one, for that is not his business. It is, however, reasonable to think that the open-endedness of *Le Cid* represents a genuine ambiguity not of form, but of substance – an ambiguity such as, in other plays of Corneille, will be found surrounding other exceptional actions.

This ambiguity is of the essence of tragedy, because it implies limitation; and it leaves us to reflect that whatever relationship the lovers may achieve, it will not be the *same* as the one they would have had if the Count had not been killed by Rodrigue, however honourably. Their innocence, at least, will have gone beyond recall, and with it the freedom from care implied by the word *Mocedades* in de Castro's title.

3

Horace

The success of *Le Cid* put Corneille at once into the forefront of the playwrights of the time. It also, however, exposed him to the jealousy of rivals in the famous controversy known as the *Querelle du Cid*, which dragged on for two years. This critical debate turned mainly on the play's alleged irregularities of structure, taste and style; and although it appears to have had no effect at all on the fortunes of the work, it led Corneille to ponder more seriously on the problems of dramatic art, with obvious benefit to his next masterpiece, *Horace*. In addition to being more regular, this differs from *Le Cid* in being unequivocally a tragedy; and it also shows him seeking a subject in Roman history, which was to remain one of his most constant sources of inspiration.

The Subject

The primary source for *Horace* is Book I (Chapters 23–26) of Livy's History of Rome, *Ab Urbe Condita*, which evokes a relatively primitive period when Rome was struggling for supremacy with the sister-city of Alba Longa, with whose population she had close ties of kinship. The pretext for this struggle – not, apparently, sufficiently dignified to be specified by Corneille – was an affair of reciprocal cattle-rustling, which turned into a war, in some respects a civil war.

The episode selected from Livy begins with the decision of the opposing leaders to settle the conflict by means of a *representative* combat involving only three champions from each side, thus opening the way to the creation of a new community with the dominating partner clearly defined; but also (as an additional motive of political expediency) preventing the possibility of a common foe dominating both of them. This plan derives from the fact that, by a quirk of fortune, the armies contain evenly-matched sets of triplet brothers: the Roman Horatii and the Alban Curiatii; and its merit is offset only by one difficult human problem, conveniently ignored by everybody: namely, that a sister of the Horatii is betrothed to one of the Curiatii.

With the agreement of the six young men, the plan is ratified and sanctified by a treaty, and a combat duly takes place which, in Livy's narration, is already of an essentially dramatic nature since it involves a major 'reversal of fortune'. At first, the Romans are placed in a disastrous situation by the killing of two of the Horatii; but in achieving this advantage the Curiatii are all wounded. The remaining and unwounded Roman, Publius Horatius, though no match for the three together, is enabled to kill them separately by resorting to the stratagem of feigned flight. The pursuing Curiatii, handicapped in different degrees by their wounds, thus fall victims of a truly Roman trick of 'divide and rule'.

On returning from the combat which has assured the future ascendancy of Rome, the exultant Horatius, loaded with the trophies of victory, is met by his sister, who, seeing on his shoulders the cloak of her betrothed, woven by herself, bursts into lamentation for her dead lover. Whereupon Horatius, exalted beyond the normal measure by personal glory and patriotic ardour, kills her too, as an exemplary punishment for a woman who could be so unmindful of the sacrifice of her brothers and her obligations to her country.

Horatius, now doubly and ironically distinguished as a hero *and* a murderer (the two things being linked in the motivation), is brought to judgement; and after some diplomatic handwashing by the king and an appeal from his father, who defends the killing of his daughter Horatia as a just act, is acquitted by a decision of the Roman people (though, as Livy is careful to point out, this is more from admiration of his bravery than persuasion of the justice of his cause). So Horatius is suffered to live in the glory of public heroism provided that his private shame is also remembered through certain expiatory rites to be perpetuated in his family.

Such is Livy's semi-legendary tale, a good story by any standards. As a source of moral conflicts and ambiguities as well as exceptional and tragic events, it would be an outstanding subject for Corneille were it not for the fact that it tends towards anticlimax at the end, and that as it stands, the action is rather thin for a full five-act tragedy. It presents, therefore, certain difficulties; and while the first of these – the risk of anticlimax – has been thought by some critics (and by Corneille himself) not to have been entirely overcome, his handling of the remainder is a striking demonstration of technical skill.

Corneille's Modification of the Subject

The Characters

Whereas with *Le Cid* Corneille has had to condense a wealth of material in order to create a dramatic crisis, his problem in *Horace* is the opposite: namely, to expand in a dramatically and psychologically satisfying way material already presented in condensed form by Livy. To do this, he first modifies the scheme of characters.

The opposing armies are reduced to two messenger-figures, Flavian and Procule; and of the two leaders only the Roman king Tulle is introduced directly. On the other hand, the role of Horace's father – *le vieil Horace* – is expanded to allow him to represent more fully the perspective of Roman patriotism within the family, and to intervene in the action before the combat. As for the combatants themselves, these are made even more 'representative' in the sense that only Horace and Curiace are actually seen on the stage, their respective brothers being merely referred to in certain narrations.

On the female side (where there is obviously scope for expansion), Horace's sister is renamed Camille, for psychological rather than linguistic reasons; and he is given a wife, Sabine, an invented character whose potential importance is indicated by the fact that she is an Alban, and sister of the Curiaces. Since she cannot affect materially the course of outward events, her role is partly one of passive suffering, to serve as an additional source and focus of *pathos*. But, merely by her presence, she also adds a new and indispensable dimension to the moral content of the play; and although at first sight she appears to make up a 'foursome' of incredible symmetry, the fact that she is *married* to Horace puts her on a completely different footing from that of Camille and constitutes a deliberate asymmetry. Camille and Sabine share a confidante, Julie; and finally, Corneille has taken aspects of certain episodic figures in Livy – a priest and the duumvirs – to work up into a new character called Valère, a Roman knight and rejected suitor of Camille. His presence offers the unfortunate girl a permanent option in the play; and in the closing stages he acts as prosecutor of Horace to balance the defending function exercised by the latter's father.

With these modifications, Corneille has set up a group of characters whose interaction offers possibilities of conflict, and extended psychological analysis sufficient to fill out the sketch of events by Livy.

The Dramatic Mechanism

In his own retrospective examination of the play (which should not be taken entirely at face-value) Corneille admits a number of defects, two of which concern directly the structure and mechanism. The first of these is that the murder of Camille which becomes the principal action, is the affair of a moment,

lacking adequate magnitude and preparation. The second is
that it creates a double action by exposing Horace to a second
and unnecessary 'peril' which, moreover, is of a lower order in
that it is a private rather than a public matter.

The first of these admissions is debatable, but the second is
nonsense, because without the second 'peril' there might be
some sort of drama but certainly not a tragedy in any profound
sense. Initially at least, the whole attraction of the subject lies
precisely in this duality, which is a source of tragic irony and an
illustration of a human paradox: that even noble aspirations
can be self-defeating, and worse. The murder, therefore, and the
resulting second peril *must* become the 'principal action'; and it
is this act, rather than the combat, which must provide the
climax of the outward events, irrespective of what may happen
afterwards. Consequently, Corneille's major technical problem
is not only to fill out a five-act structure but to do it in such a
way as to make a repugnant act *credible* as well as 'true', and
without destroying all sympathy for the nominal 'hero' Horace.
He must, in short, interest and excite the audience, stimulate
varied emotional responses such as pity, fear, contempt or
admiration; and finally dismiss it in reflective mood – and all
this within a conventional scheme which rejects direct violence.

In response to this challenge, Corneille has produced an
expository first act containing only three appropriately slow-
moving scenes. Because of the paucity of outward events
available to him, no major physical action is possible at this
stage; but the act is still dramatic in a number of ways. First,
it conveys the basic situation at a moment of *suspense*, when
hostilities between Rome and Alba have been halted by the plan
for a representative combat, but the choice of champions has
not been made. The prevailing tension is skilfully conveyed
through the emotions of the women characters, beginning with
the frustration and misery of Sabine who, in expressing
pathetically the conflict of public and private loyalties, estab-
lishes at once a mood of foreboding.

At the same time – and this is one of the original features of the play – it is made clear that the women cannot really stand together in their common distress, because of an element of mutual jealousy and mistrust. Sabine, an older woman who has little freedom of action because of her married status, suspects Camille of wavering in her loyalty to the absent Curiace and of encouraging Valère, the Roman; but her attempt to probe into this through the agency of Julie provokes an almost hysterical affirmation of loyalty from Camille, which finds an outlet in the third and final scene of the act, when Curiace actually appears, having profited from the truce to visit his Roman lover. Camille clings to him possessively as her 'plus unique bien' (v. 141), in a way which suggests adolescent insecurity as well as love; and the act concludes on a suitable note of tension and the customary foreshadowing of the denouement, with the lovers poised between hope of an early union and fear that the conflict between their respective cities will finally come between them.

Apart from necessary information about the situation between Rome and Alba, the material of Act I is the invention of Corneille; and one of its most important and necessary functions is to initiate a cumulative process of *exasperation* which, working on the sensibilities of the still immature Camille, must finally bring about the disastrous confrontation with her brother Horace, who has not yet actually appeared in the play. Despite Corneille's subsequent self-criticism, the spring of this tragedy is already being tightened – and very skilfully.

In Act II, as might be expected, the psychological action is considerably advanced, although the main physical events must still be delayed. The first striking feature of the act is a change of perspective in the early scenes, through a shift of emphasis to the principal male protagonists, and the introduction of Horace's father as a senior representative of Roman patriotism. The second is a clear division of male and female characters in their attitude to the situation.

The main dramatic interest of the act derives from the choice of combatants, and must do so because the source-material offers nothing else that can be exploited at this stage without weakening the later phases of the action. Corneille does, however, change the story in one significant detail: namely, that whereas in Livy the idea of the representative combat is suggested by the fortuitous presence of the two sets of triplets, he has made their nomination a matter of deliberate choice consequent upon an agreement in principle to resolve the conflict in this way. This confers on the protagonists at the outset a greater degree of distinction; and, psychologically, makes it almost impossible for them to back out of what each accepts as social obligation, albeit with differing degrees of enthusiasm.

Horace's sense of honour and personal *gloire* is revealed at his first appearance in Scene 1, by his reaction to the news of his selection and the diplomatic comments of Curiace thereon. If he should die, he wants no tears to be shed:

> Mais quoique ce combat me promette un cercueil,
> La gloire de ce choix m'enfle d'un juste orgueil;
>
> (vv. 377–8)

In Scene 2, however, the situation changes and tension rises with the announcement that Curiace and his brothers have been named for Alba; and in Scene 3 the contrast of temperaments (already hinted at) emerges clearly in the violent protests uttered by Curiace even as he accepts his dubious honour. This is, indeed, the point in the play where the thematic distinction is fully established between what is 'Roman' and what is 'human' – the claims of the state and the claims of the individual. The patriotism of Horace now rises to the level of transcendent religious obligation:

> Ce droit saint et sacré rompt tout autre lien.
> Rome a choisi mon bras, je n'examine rien:
>
> (vv. 497–8)

and in the face of this dedication, the human sensibility of Curiace is likely to prove fatal, as he himself seems to be saying in the famous exchange

> HORACE: Albe vous a nommé, je ne vous connais plus.
> CURIACE: Je vous connais encore, et c'est ce qui me tue.
> (vv. 502–3)

Scene 4 of this act is very short, but of crucial importance in the chain of circumstances leading to the murder because in it Horace, looking ahead to the possible consequences of the new situation (and he is the only one who really does this in detail), tries to impress on Camille the absolute necessity of accepting with equal fortitude the death of either brothers or lover which must be the outcome of the combat. There is, as will be seen later, a superb irony in the opening of his speech to her:

> Armez-vous de constance, *et montrez-vous ma sœur;*
> (v. 517)

But it is essential to our understanding of him to realize that he does *not* forbid her in advance to *lament* whoever may be killed (which is all that she does in Livy's account). He is not by nature that inhuman. What he does try to insist upon, knowing Camille's temperament, is that she shall not *reproach* whoever turns out to be the victor; for he will only have done his duty. In this apparently trivial point, there is a significant difference between Corneille and Livy.

The remainder of Act II is devoted to further development of the domestic repercussions of the choice of combatants, as both Camille and Sabine – united for once – try to shake the determination of their menfolk to go through with what for the women is pure barbarity. The means employed are appropriate to the characters: i.e. direct emotional pleading by Camille and, as befits a more mature woman, a more sophisticated form of moral pressure by Sabine, who produces some quite remarkable dialectics in an attempt to persuade them that only if they were to kill her first could their combat have any semblance of rational justification. In the face of her threat to intervene in it, both Curiace and Horace show signs of weakening, and the situation is saved for them only by the elder Horace who, though emotionally torn himself, urges them to do their duty to their respective cities, and undertakes to prevent the women from intervening. At this stage, therefore, the attitudes of the characters have been defined and the combat can take place.

In the classic five-act structure Act III is apt to present special difficulties because of the need to sustain interest without anticipating the main climax. Here, as it happens, Corneille faces an unusually difficult problem because while the story itself now focuses attention on the famous fight, the dramatic conventions require this to be reported and not seen. His solution of it is to make the reporting of the combat itself the source of additional dramatic interest through its effect on Sabine, Camille and the elder Horace; and the device which he uses is simply to divide the narration into three phases shared between three characters, the first two of whom convey incomplete or misleading information. Thus, without lessening the interest of the fight, he can intensify the parallel drama which must take place if the murder of Camille is to be satisfactorily explained. Moreover, by constructing the entire third act around the incomplete reports, he can produce an alternation between hopes and fears and a minor climax, while reserving the full story of events for the build-up of his major climax.

Act III opens quietly, therefore, with a time-filling monologue by Sabine which, with appropriate pathos, gathers together and projects forward all the insoluble problems of conflicting loyalties. But this lull is broken by the intervention of Julie who, in Scene 2, heightens the suspense by telling Sabine that the combat has been delayed by the revulsion of the armies from such a spectacle. However, since the combatants themselves are unwilling to renounce the honour which they deem to have been conferred on them, the leaders have decided to test the will of the Gods by a ritual sacrifice. Now this particular 'reversal of fortune' is invented by Corneille, and like most of his departures from Livy is extremely important for the psychological drama. It means that at a moment when a drawing-back seems possible, not only Horace but *all six* combatants refuse to return to the level of common humanity, being overcome by a sense of tragic privilege and that *juste orgueil* (or vanity) expressed earlier by Horace. In this there is a fine example of Corneille's insight into group-behaviour.

The reaction of the women to this news is interesting and typical. In Scene 3, still in the restraining presence of Julie, Sabine talks of *hope*, and Camille counters with expressions of *despair*. In Scene 4, however, after Julie's departure to seek further news, their mutual antipathy breaks out again into a sort of competition in suffering, in which Sabine claims that the situation is worse for her as the actual wife of Horace than it is for Camille who, being merely betrothed, is free to renounce Curiace and find another love (presumably Valère). To this Camille replies, with the cruel and possibly truthful contempt of youth:

> Je le vois bien, ma sœur, vous n'aimâtes jamais.
>
> (v. 917)

It is now clear, therefore, that the struggle of Rome and Alba is not confined to the warriors; a parallel conflict is going on between the women, and the exasperation of Camille in particular has been advanced a further step.

To cut short this unseemly quarrel and provide a new focus of interest, Corneille now completes his act with two scenes in which the limelight passes to the elder Horace. In Scene 5, he reports that with the approval of the Gods the combat is actually taking place, and, exalted by his own faith in the destiny of Rome, counsels both women to commit themselves completely to the Roman cause; but, by another 'reversal of fortune', his superb confidence is immediately shattered by the return of Julie (Scene 6) to report the death of two of his sons and the flight of the third which, seen from a distance, has been taken to be the end of the affair. It is under this misapprehension that he pronounces the famous condemnation of Horace: *Qu'il mourût. . . .* (v. 1021), and departs breathing destruction for a son believed to have shamed both family and nation.

Since the climax is obviously at hand, there can be no interval before Act IV, in which the dramatic rhythm is brilliantly sustained. First (with another stroke of irony) Camille pleads with her father to relent; but is immediately overtaken by events, in that Valère appears in Scene 2 with a full and accurate account of the fight, including Horace's final victory. This *récit* (vv. 1103–40) is the great 'set piece' of the text, punctuated by a single *Hélas!* from Camille, in which there is more pathos than in the entire narrative which it interrupts. This recital is, of course, closely modelled on the source-material; but again, Corneille has subtly modified Livy's account, with two objects in mind. The first is to penetrate beyond the killings to the actual thoughts and motives of the combatants (this being an advantage of the classical technique of narration over mere physical spectacle); and the second is to present the victorious Horace not as braver or stronger than his opponents, but as a fighter at once more *intelligent* and more *inspired* by the religious quality of Roman patriotism. In the first case, he has invented for the Curiaces such 'human' motives as indignation or the desire for vengeance, while retaining for Horace the almost ritualistic motivation to be found in Livy. In the second, he has re-thought and rationalized the actual movements of the battle, allowing Horace to wait to be attacked instead of rushing *back* to the Curiaces, thus losing part of the advantage

gained in flight. His victory is indeed one of tactics rather than
force, and his killings are, technically, either defensive or
ritualistic – a point which demonstrates the remarkable intellectual grip which Corneille has on his subject.

This, then, is the moment of climax, especially for Horace's
father; but in this scheme of irony, it is for Camille the moment
of catastrophe, the impact of which is heightened by the old
man's insensitivity. In Scene 3 – short, like so many crucial
ones – he points out to his daughter, with monumental inepti-
tude, that Curiace was, after all, only a man; that Rome has
plenty of substitutes to offer; that Sabine – *Sabine*, the Alban
woman! – has more cause for tears than Camille; and that she,
Camille, should receive Horace in a way worthy of his and the
family's new glory, and as a true sister.

> Faites-vous voir sa sœur, et qu'en un même flanc
> Le ciel vous a tous deux formés d'un même sang.
>
> (vv. 1193–4)

With this pontifical addition to the nagging previously inflicted
on her by Julie and Sabine, Camille's exasperation is now
almost at its peak; and it only remains for her to complete the
pattern of savage irony and paradox by showing that she is
indeed the sister of Horace and joint inheritor of the family
temperament, but taking up a defiant position at the contrary
extreme, and asserting her own individuality by denying the
values of her father and brother. Her great monologue in Scene
4 shows her 'working up' to the inevitable confrontation:

> Dégénérons, mon cœur, d'un si vertueux père;
> Soyons indigne sœur d'un si généreux frère:
>
> (vv. 1239–40)

In this way, Corneille prepares a memorable encounter,
charged with the concerted energy of extreme indignation and

extreme exaltation, both comprehensible, both reprehensible in that they lead to an automatism of emotion or reason.

In a scene (5) invested with symbolic significance by the presence of the three swords of the dead Curiaces, Horace, strained and exalted in his *gloire* and temporarily unable to distinguish between state and individual, checks even the tears which, before the combat, he would have allowed Camille to shed, thus driving her himself to utter the 'reproaches' which he has foreseen and tried to forbid. The result is not only a denunciation of his 'brutality', but the famous blasphemy against Rome itself:

> l'unique objet de mon ressentiment! (v. 1301)

a prophecy of destruction and invocation of civil war, cut short with the equally famous sword-thrust, and Horace's succinct utterance:

> C'est trop, ma patience à la *raison* fait place;
> Va dedans les enfers plaindre ton Curiace.
> (vv. 1319–20)

followed by a last *Ah! traître!* from the dying Camille, the precise sense of which is still debatable.

So ends the main dramatic action, leaving, as material for the last two scenes of Act IV and the whole of Act V, the judgement of Horace and the problem of adjustment to the new circumstances on both the private and the public plane. Since Horace is again in peril of his life, the play's conclusion offers the same interest as modern 'courtroom drama'; and Corneille is able to prolong the play because Horace can and must be judged twice: privately by his father and publicly by the state. In the first case he is spared on grounds of expediency, as the sole survivor of his father's children; and in the second, reasons of state also lead to a pardon on similar grounds of expediency, despite his willingness to die in order to preserve intact his glory as saviour of the state and virtual founder of a new political establishment.

Although amplified by Corneille through the full use of different characters, the ending follows the general line of Livy's account, leaving us to conclude that Horace is in effect punished *morally*, by being condemned to *live* in an equivocal situation which denies him the satisfaction of a 'pure' act, unless and until time shall bring its own healing and reconciliation. The line of logic being worked out in this ambiguous way, only love can provide hope for the future; and this, indeed, seems to be the message of the King's final speech, which invites Horace and Valère to effect a reconciliation.

The Characters and Themes of the Play

The foregoing summary of Corneille's reworking indicates his skill as a playwright concerned to give psychological depth to Livy's silhouettes; but it cannot give a complete view of the *themes* as distinct from the *subject*. To obtain a better view of what the play is about, other angles of approach are possible, the first of which is provided by the characters themselves who, naturally, represent in their actions certain fundamental ideas and attitudes.

First, Horace himself is apparently the 'total Roman' imagined by men of letters: the uncompromising patriot, ready not only to sacrifice all to the state, but to do it without question and to find his greatest satisfaction in so doing. This view of him is obviously justified by certain sections of the text, the best-known being, perhaps,

> J'accepte aveuglément cette gloire avec joie.   (v. 492)

As a corollary to this, however, it is often assumed that he has no ordinary human sensibility, this being indicated by the formal contrast between *Romain* and *humain*, *Rome* and *homme*,

which recurs frequently enough to assume thematic significance.
It should be remembered, nevertheless, that there are few good
rhymes for *Rome* and *Romain*, and that the apparent exclusive-
ness of these antitheses may derive from the exigencies of versi-
fication. For, considered apart from the combat itself, Horace
is not insensitive. He does not deny that the situation is one of
malheur:

> Notre malheur est grand; il est au plus haut point;
> Je l'envisage *entier*, mais je n'en frémis point: (489–90)

And he is not blind either, except in the sense of *choosing* not to
look at certain things. On the contrary, he is the most far-
sighted of the combatants, and his tragedy is that at a crucial
moment his far-sightedness will not allow him to focus properly
on what is under his nose: namely, the suffering of a distraught
and emotional girl. A patriot Horace certainly is; but he must
not be taken for an unthinking patriot or, as critics have
sometimes suggested, a 'brute beast' or mere killer. It is because
he is the opposite of a brute beast that he commits an act which,
outwardly, is indistinguishable from that of a beast.

Curiace is a patriot too, equally determined to do his duty;
but he is still a reluctant patriot. Being emotional and impulsive
by temperament – (Combien contre le ciel il vomit de blas-
phèmes! v. 180) – and incapable of the objectivity of Horace, he
is condemned to failure through the attractive weakness of
being unable to forget personal relationships. Inevitably, he
attracts compassion, particularly from modern audiences, and
it is easy to assume that Corneille wished it so and that his own
sympathies are with Curiace.

In certain respects, these male adversaries are balanced by
the female pair Sabine–Camille. Sabine, an Alban herself, is
naturally opposed to 'Roman' qualities when carried to
extremes; and living with Horace has apparently sharpened
her wits to the point where she can usually get the better of her

husband in an argument. She also plays a part in the goading of Camille; yet she remains a victim of circumstances, a pathetic figure in whose tears, restrained at the beginning (v. 13) and shed at the end (v. 1769), the whole tragedy of war is reflected.

Camille is an excellent example of the complexities of Cornelian characterization. At first sight, as the upholder of love against patriotism, she seems diametrically opposed to her brother; yet it turns out that the opposition is less in the characters themselves than in the values to which they are committed respectively. In the last analysis, Camille is what her father bids her to be – one of the Roman Horatii – even though the only way of proving it is to go on challenging the others to the bitter end. Her death is therefore conceivable as, amongst other things, a punishment for the elder Horace who, although partly mellowed by age, is still capable of the same ruthless devotion to principle as his offspring. And it is for this reason that the study of the characters suggests as one important tragic theme, apart from the conflict of love and patriotism, the idea of a family destroying itself by its own energy, extremism and inflexibility of temperament. It has been argued, indeed, that the title *Horace* has a certain ambiguity about it, and that the 'tragic hero' of the play is collective rather than individual.

Even when they are reduced to the simple terms given above, the characters can obviously lead directly to some of the ideas behind the play. On the other hand, there are some themes and ideas of a more philosophical nature which it is profitable to consider separately because of the light which they can throw in turn on the characters.

The central theme is the traditional and universal one of human limitation, and of attempts made to overcome it; and Corneille's treatment of it shows that in *Horace* the conflicts are much more than a clash of personalities, and that the characterization is less clear-cut than it might seem. What this involves, fundamentally, is a series of moral and political paradoxes linked at various levels with the idea of *parricide*, the term being used broadly to indicate both the killing of relatives and treason. The word itself occurs regularly in the text, with various connotations, and the most obvious example of the act is, of course, the killing of sister by brother which forms the climax. But the whole conflict between Rome and Alba is itself a collective *parricide*, in that there is a common element in the legendary origins of the cities as reported, for example, by Livy. Moreover Romulus, the reputed founder of Rome, was of Alban stock, and owes his special place in Roman legend partly to the fact that he slew his twin brother Remus in the course of a jealous affray. This, too, is mentioned in the play, and it suggests that one point which Corneille has seized upon in Livy is that the origins of Rome are tainted. Another is that the particular struggle which he has chosen to dramatize represents only one phase – albeit a crucial one – in a political evolution, an inexorable historical process, by which a society organizes itself as an entity, and a new order is formed with its own sense of political identity, its own moral and even religious outlook, superseding a system of loose and primitive clan-loyalties which is, no doubt, more 'natural', but is fraught nevertheless with internecine violence. As a matter of history, such evolutions may and do take place, but almost always at a price of human suffering during the transitional phase, such as Corneille has depicted in *Horace*. What is involved, is the passage from the rule of force to the rule of convention; and the peculiarly tragic status of the Horaces and the Curiaces collectively derives from the fact that they are caught up in the chain of events at a halfway stage, when the aspirations of Rome are still conceivable as no more than greed for power.

Before the opening of the play, there has been a state of general conflict in comparison with which the acceptance of a representative battle marks the beginning of a rule of convention. Nevertheless, the original motive behind this plan is still one of expediency, related to calculations of force. It is in fact proposed by the *Alban* leader as a measure of reason in the common interest, but only to direct aggressiveness – 'l'ambition de commander aux autres' (v. 303) – elsewhere. Now it may be thought a better thing that a few should die rather than many, in order to settle a political issue; but strictly speaking the improvement in the situation is statistical or *quantitative* rather than *qualitative*. The predominance of Rome or Alba is still to be decided by force, and the outcome must be as harsh for the select minority as it would have been for the majority who can now retire to the sidelines as spectators. *Horace* is therefore conceivable in the first place as the tragedy of a small group suffering for a majority; but since the advantage envisaged for the majority is still crudely political, the *value* of the suffering remains in doubt. It is in fact up to each individual member of the minority to create or extract such moral value as he can out of suffering, and the ultimate poignancy and irony of the play lies in the fact that the attempts to do so give rise to mutually destructive forms of personal idealism and *gloire*; and a situation of what might be called moral *parricide*, in addition to the physical and political *parricide* which makes up the general background.

This, therefore, is the situation within which there arises between Curiace and Horace the issue of basic human decency against the specialized virtues of Roman patriotism – both of them 'good' but, unfortunately, incompatible in the particular historical circumstances. At first sight, Curiace seems to have an ethical superiority because of his obvious sensibility; but this depends on the point of view of the beholder, and is open to dispute. What is less disputable is the realism and intelligence of Horace, whose historical vision is such as to persuade him that future good may come out of present evil, in a world to be dominated by Rome. In the meantime, however, the suffering is real, and the only way for the minority to rise above it and create value for themselves out of it is to stand together in a sort of contract of reciprocal loyalty and respect. This is the sense of his warning to Camille before the combat; and he is probably right. Unfortunately, he could only be declared so by the tribunal of history, and it is from the anticipation of this that he derives that extreme satisfaction of patriotic *gloire* which proves his undoing when it becomes too personalized, and shows him as both a better and a worse man than Curiace. For thus does Corneille point the theme of human limitation, with an exemplary demonstration of self-defeating idealism.

In the historical and philosophical perspectives which Corneille has provided for his play, it is possible to respect Horace for his energy and intelligence, but it is still difficult to regard a man who kills his sister in a fit of 'reason' as anything but a dangerous fanatic. Yet even fanatics do have their reasons, like other men; and seeing this, Corneille is subtle enough to have made it not quite impossible to view both the fanaticism and the murder with compassion, by putting Horace into situations in which he is, despite appearances, more vulnerable than the 'human' Curiace.

In the first place, he is tragically committed from the outset in that he is actually married to an Alban. In other words, his private life is already under the rule of reason and contract going beyond the boundaries of the state, whereas there is as yet no equivalent public relationship between the two cities. For him, therefore, there can be no private peace until the public conflict is resolved, whereas Curiace is still technically and legally a free agent, at least as far as Camille is concerned. This is why Horace sees the *malheur* as *entier*, and why his way of meeting it must be no less 'entire'; and it is for this reason, as well as through patriotic idealism, that his acceptance of the duty to fight is deemed by him to be 'blind'. If it were not, his situation would be unbearable.

As for the murder, the 'blasphemy' of Camille which provokes it seems genuinely intolerable to him, not just as a personal affront, nor as an absurd denial of history, but as a negation of the value of a desperate combat in which not only their brothers but Curiace himself have just died. Her prophecy of, and wish for, Rome's self-destruction is tantamount to willing the resumption of the vicious circle of general *parricide* which the restricted *parricide* of the combat is supposed to be ending, so that the whole thing will have been gone through for nothing. In anathematizing Rome, therefore (a new Rome, let us remember), she is denying the value of five men's lives and a sixth man's anguish, as well as glory; and this is why, despite his own faults, Horace's 'reason' condemns her to death as a *monstre*, and cannot recant. It can be argued, in fact, that Camille 'murders' Horace in a moral sense before he murders her in a physical sense. Hence their father's agreement that the punishment is just, although Horace has no right to be judge or executioner; and hence also the possibility of pity for the tainted glory of one of the saddest of Corneille's heroes.

4

Cinna

Since Corneille's next play was conceived at about the same time as *Horace* and staged in the same year, 1640, it may be expected to show some continuity or resemblance of general inspiration. Continuity is indeed seen in the choice of another Roman subject; but the possibility of further resemblance seems restricted by the fact that the events depicted directly or indirectly in *Cinna* do not include actual violence. In the long run this must raise interesting general questions about the nature of tragedy; but a more immediate and particular problem posed by *Cinna* concerns the subject itself.

The Subject

At first sight, this seems straightforward enough. Cinna is the name of a young man who plotted to assassinate the emperor Augustus; and the play tells a simple story of the discovery of the plot and the emperor's decision not to put him to death. The title suggests therefore that Cinna is to be the central figure or hero of a drama, if not of a tragedy; but this is not quite borne out by Corneille's treatment, because half-way through the play the focus of interest shifts from the actions of Cinna to the reactions of Augustus. The importance of this is underlined by the fact that in 1643 Corneille gave the first printed edition of the work the double title of *Cinna ou la clémence d'Auguste*; and it means that not only the tragic nature of the play but also the status of the characters is open to discussion. For these reasons *Cinna* is, if not quite the greatest, at any rate one of the most interesting of all Corneille's productions; and the first step to the appreciation of it is, as usual, to trace the processes of invention, beginning with the source-material.

The origin of the work is an anecdote from Seneca's moral essay on Mercy (*De Clementia*) reproduced in slightly garbled form in an essay by Montaigne, whose sixteenth-century French version was included in the first edition, and has continued to accompany Corneille's text. This version tells us simply that when in Gaul, Augustus was informed of the plot of Cinna, a grandson of Pompey the Great and therefore a kind of hereditary enemy, on whom, nevertheless, he had showered favours. After spending a sleepless night debating with himself whether or not to have the young man executed, the emperor was persuaded by his wife Livia to reverse the established practice, which had never succeeded in stamping out conspiracies, and to try the effect of clemency. Having accepted this advice and reduced the punishment of Cinna to a humiliating interview, followed in due course by further favours, Augustus found that these tactics did pay a political dividend, and was never troubled again by such conspiracies. This outline story is accompanied by a few circumstantial details, followed fairly closely by Corneille.

A second source used by him is the Roman History of the third-century writer Cassius Dio (Book LII, 1–40), which contains a political discussion and a debate on abdication which took place between Augustus and his friends Maecenas and Agrippa. This provides the substance of Act II, Scene 1; and it is probable that Corneille consulted other passages of Cassius Dio: e.g. Book LV, 14–22, which gives a variant of the main story; and perhaps Book LIII, 16, which discusses the circumstances and significance of the assumption by the emperor of the name Augustus, and may have a direct bearing on Corneille's themes. Although Cassius Dio is regarded as a minor source, he must not be overlooked, because he provides, amongst other things, a time-scale against which we can set Corneille's play and judge certain aspects of his creative achievement. For example, the discussion of abdication took place in 29 B.C.; the taking of the title 'Augustus' (which signifies something sacred or more than human, worthy of reverence) belongs to 27 B.C.; but the conspiracy dramatized by Corneille did not occur, according to Cassius Dio, until A.D. 4, and in Rome rather than Gaul. All this means that Corneille has carried out on Roman history an operation like that which his predecessor de Castro had performed on the legends of the Cid, in order to produce a drama of moral crisis into which is distilled a lifetime of political experience on the part of Augustus, the 'master of the universe'. This confers on *Cinna* a remarkable power of expansion in the mind, and is one of the factors which compensate for the absence of violence in the play itself.

Finally, it is customary, when examining the sources of the play, to mention the political atmosphere of seventeenth-century France, because the period of Richelieu abounds with conspiracies, punished with extreme severity; and the writing of *Cinna* coincided with a peasant revolt in Corneille's native province of Normandy, also met with severe repression. It would, however, be hazardous to deduce from these events that Corneille was giving Richelieu a lesson in statesmanship, though his play could have considerable box-office appeal when it was written.

Such, then, are Corneille's known and possible sources of inspiration; and taken together they confirm that the work has two major aspects which must be treated convergently. These are identified by Corneille in his dedication of the work to Montoron in 1643 as 'une ingratitude extraordinaire' and 'un extraordinaire effort de clémence', both of which must be explained. And although these aspects are ultimately inseparable, they pose quite different problems for the playwright. In all that relates to Augustus, his task is mainly to concentrate and assemble in the most dramatically effective way material selected from a fairly wide range of historical testimony; but in relation to Cinna, about whom the sources say very little, he must *invent* enough material to fill out a five-act play, just as he had to do in the case of Camille. In this process he must, however, observe three conditions: first, he has to provide adequate motivation for Cinna's betrayal of his benefactor; secondly – since this is a conspiracy that failed – he has to provide reasons for this, and in particular, for the revelation of it to the emperor; and thirdly, he must inject into the conspiracy enough moral content to feed the dilemma of the emperor, which the sources already show to have been of a moral as well as a political nature. To do all these things and create a play, Corneille sets up first of all an appropriate character-scheme, as he has done in *Horace*.

The Scheme of Characters

Augustus, on whom the limelight eventually falls, is broadly in accordance with the testimony used by Corneille, but it is essential for an understanding of the play to remember that he has had in view the whole of the emperor's career. This means that the imperial figure depicted by him is really *two men in one*, in the sense that within 'Augustus' there still survives, to some extent, his original personality as *Octavian*, who has advanced to his Principate by every kind of political ruse or violence. It is this past career of Octavian which provides such justification as exists for the conspiracy; and the beauty of Corneille's dramatic mechanism (as well as the themes of the play) depends at almost every step upon this dual personality.

In the case of Cinna, Corneille has almost a free hand, because the sources tell him only two things, the first of which is that Cinna was a descendant of Pompey. This, however, does not suffice in the play to explain his role as conspirator; but it does help Corneille to develop allusions to the background of civil war and violence which are essential to his major themes. Apart from this, the sources reveal only that Cinna was a rather incompetent young man (*stolidi ingenii* – 'dull-witted' – is Seneca's term for him, though this is not in the Montaigne version); so that Corneille's task here has been to create not only a rounded and fully-motivated character, but a partially sympathetic one. In short, Cinna becomes – and must become – just enough of an *honnête homme* to have genuine moral problems of his own and to pose a genuine problem for the emperor.

It is the necessity of motivating Cinna adequately which has provided the greatest challenge to Corneille's inventiveness; and he has taken advantage of the opportunity by creating two major characters, Emilie and Maxime, who, within their general role as conspirators, have separate problems and separate dramatic functions.

Emilie is in fact the mainspring of the whole conspiracy, since it is she who has sworn vengeance on the emperor for the death of her father. She is loved by Cinna, whose part in the affair is dictated mainly by his passion, which is stronger than the obligation that each of them has towards Augustus who, in reparation for the past, has become almost a father to them both. Emilie therefore takes over the inspirational role, in accordance with her personal qualities of energy, courage and pride; and Cinna is reduced to a kind of 'front man' – a role which, while not devoid of idealism, is nevertheless more in keeping with historical testimony as to his character, and renders him more pathetic than heroic. Consequently, the woman in the affair seems more 'virile' than the men, an apparent incongruity which is usually justified by reference to a number of such characters who actually existed in Corneille's time – e.g. Mme de Chevreuse.

Maxime, though appearing at first as a sincere champion of Roman liberty, is nevertheless the least sympathetic character, and must be so since, functionally, he exists mainly to provide the weak link and betray the conspiracy. The reason for this in the play is jealousy of Cinna, for, as is revealed rather late in the action, he too is in love with Emilie, and his selfish desires expose him to the ignoble persuasions of his freedman Euphorbe. The role of Maxime is perhaps the least satisfactory aspect of the play, but it is dictated largely by dramatic necessities. It should also be said, in justice to Corneille, that he has managed the problem of motivation in a most economical and *efficient* way, by making desire for Emilie a reason for both the rise and the fall of the conspiracy.

Apart from the usual confidants, Corneille has completed his character-scheme by taking over from the sources the emperor's wife Livia who, in addition to providing a domestic background, has to perform one vital function: namely, to suggest that the conspirators be pardoned as a measure of political expediency. However, in Corneille's version, where there is more concern for the motives than for the act, Livia's contribution is more subtle and has a different significance in relation to the themes of the play.

The Dramatic Mechanism

Given these characters, Corneille's next technical problem, as in *Horace*, is to derive from their relationships a set of actions converging to produce an extraordinary event: the emperor's decision to show mercy. This, therefore, forms the conclusion of the play; and the only other major external event he can exploit is the betrayal of the plot. So, this 'reversal of fortune' becomes inevitably the hinge or turning-point of the play, to which the first three acts lead up, and of which the last two acts show the consequences. To fill out the first part, Corneille can legitimately analyse the relationships of three people; but in the second part he needs a delaying-device. This he provides by making the betrayal both misleading and incomplete, so allowing for a gradual revelation of the *whole* truth by the three conspirators. This is the prerequisite for the emperor's final decision, the inward significance of which does not fully emerge until the very last line of the play:

... Auguste a tout appris et veut tout oublier.

(v. 1780)

The first step towards this totality of experience and com-
prehension is, of course, a general exposition introducing
some of the leading characters. This is provided by Act I,
which opens, rather unusually, with a soliloquy by Emilie, an
already archaic exposition-device used by Corneille on this
occasion because the bi-polarity of his subject necessitates
at the outset a clear statement of the position at one of the
extremes.

This speech offers therefore the historical perspective which
appears to justify Emilie's claim for vengeance; but it also
expresses emotional conflict over the risk of death for the lover
who must be the instrument of the desired vengeance. It is thus
dramatic in itself, and ends with a characteristically Cornelian
affirmation of purpose and principle:

Amour, sers mon devoir, et ne le combats plus:
Lui céder, c'est ta gloire, et le vaincre, ta honte ...

(vv. 48–9)

Needless to say, this extreme position is established at the
beginning partly to be attacked and tested; and the three
remaining scenes of the act all contribute to this process, with
considerable dramatic movement and fluctuation. In Scene 2,
Emilie's confidante Fulvie suggests (in typically 'unheroic'
fashion) that the benefits she has received from Auguste might
be deemed to cancel the obligation of vengeance, and that
she might leave assassination to others with similar griev-
ances. This, however, only stiffens Emilie's resolve to make
this a personal affair, capable, if all goes well, of satisfying the
claims of both duty *and* love. In Scene 3 Cinna arrives with a
powerful account of his success in stirring up the enthusiasm of
their supporters in the plan to overthrow the tyrant. As

Corneille admitted subsequently, this is a 'rhetorical adorn-
ment', but it serves the essential purpose of filling out the
exposition with a moving evocation of a long and bloody background of civil strife, and sets up a vision of Cinna poised for
the act which, according to the outcome, will establish him in
history either as a parricide or as a liberator. At this point,
however, it is announced (Scene 4) that Cinna and Maxime
have both been summoned to the imperial presence – a *coup de
théâtre* which brings the act to a very effective conclusion by
adding to the exaltation of the lovers in their commitment to
love and liberty a note of powerful suspense arising from the
possibility that Auguste has already had wind of the plot. The
rather slow opening monologue is therefore justified retro-
spectively as part of a crescendo-effect, building up to a confrontation of the emperor and the two male conspirators.

So far, everything has been disposed by Corneille in such a
way as to direct interest and sympathy towards Cinna and
Emilie, as ardent lovers and youthful idealists; but Act II
offers a dramatic reversal coupled with an unusual *rallentando*
effect. It consists, exceptionally, of only two scenes, of which the
first is Corneille's famous adaptation of Augustus's discussion
of abdication with Maecenas and Agrippa, and the second
shows the first reactions of the conspirators to a changed
situation.

The first 'deliberation scene' is of a type which is fairly
traditional but apt to provoke resistance nowadays because of
its formality and its length. It should be noted, therefore, to
Corneille's credit that it contains a brilliant condensation of
source-material running to something like fifty pages in Cassius
Dio, and that it is at the same time a superb stroke of dramatic
irony, the effect of which is actually enhanced by its length
because it is *cumulative*. The irony derives from the fact that the
monstrous tyrant evoked at the beginning of the play is here
shown from a different angle as a human being: a man who,
having achieved his ambition, is weary of the cares and alarms

inseparable from supreme political power. Seeking peace of
mind, and ignorant that his 'friends' are plotting against him in
their turn, he invites their counsel and actually offers to
abdicate in order to restore the republican liberties which the
conspirators are ostensibly striving for. Then, as though this
basic irony of situation were not enough, Corneille caps it by
making Maxime, the less estimable of the two advisers, argue
the case for abdication in the sincere belief that this will meet
the claims of the conspirators, while the more idealistic Cinna
is placed in the utterly false and hypocritical position of having
to advise the emperor to retain power in order to guarantee the
continuation of a public pretext for an assassination which he
does not really want to carry out anyway, but for which the over-
riding motive, in his case, is a private one. The arguments solemnly
propounded on each side are as respectable as the authority
of Cassius Dio can make them; but everything in the scene is
shot through with irony in relation either to the existing situation or to events still in the future. And needless to say, the
speeches have a direct bearing on the themes of the play, as in
the case of Cinna's

Il est beau de mourir maître de l'univers.   (v. 440)

countered by Maxime's

Il est beau de mourir maître de l'univers;
Mais la plus belle mort souille notre mémoire,
Quand nous avons pu vivre et croître notre gloire.
                                        (vv. 496–8)

Finally, in this scene, the play of irony reaches its climax when
the emperor decides to retain power on the advice of Cinna, and
almost in the same breath nominates Maxime as governor of
Sicily, and announces that he will marry Emilie to Cinna. The
line dividing tragedy from high comedy can seldom have been
so finely drawn.

In the face of this, and in the disarray of the moment, all that Cinna can do (Scene 2) is to cling to his private motive for assassination, leaving Maxime in a state of bewilderment which closes the act on another note of suspense – the question being this time: will the conspirators part company?

In Act II Corneille has achieved three things: first, he has introduced most effectively the second 'pole' of the action in the shape of Auguste and his problem; secondly, he has begun to direct sympathy towards the emperor; and finally, he has begun to confuse and undermine the cause of the conspirators. He has only to develop this third movement to be sure of sustaining interest in Act III, which is concerned wholly – and logically – with the further effects of Auguste's decisions upon all the conspirators in turn.

First, it is shown that Maxime is also in love with Emilie, and thus has a private motive for working against Cinna (Scene 1). Secondly (Scene 2), Maxime presses Cinna to continue with the plan for assassination, but only in order to create an opportunity to betray him. Thirdly, in his private irresolution, Cinna transfers the onus of decision to Emilie; but when faced with her intransigence, qualifies his capitulation to her stronger will with a threat to commit suicide after the assassination, in order to preserve his honour (Scenes 3 and 4). Finally (Scene 5), Emilie is depicted in a moment of conflict – distressed for her lover, but determined to maintain her demands on him. By this means, Corneille prolongs at least the possibility of sympathy for the conspirators, leaving it to be seen whether Cinna will play out his assassin's role, or simply expose himself to betrayal.

Act IV opens with the 'betrayal-scene' which is absolutely necessary to the dramatic mechanism, as Euphorbe, Maxime's freedman and spokesman, reveals to Auguste that Cinna and Maxime have plotted against him. Here begins, therefore, the gradual enlightenment of the emperor, which will be skilfully prolonged until almost the end of the play. But here also begins the actual disintegration of the conspiracy, as Euphorbe pins the major blame on Cinna, and provides for his master a way of escape through repentance. One significant point in Auguste's first reaction is that he is prepared already to pardon Maxime in view of his alleged repentance. In fact, he is prevented from doing so by Euphorbe's false report of his master's suicide; and this temporary check to external action is the occasion for the introduction, in Scene 2, of the great soliloquy which reveals the renewal of the emperor's private miseries, now redoubled in the light of Euphorbe's statements. This enables Corneille to direct attention to the moral drama which from now on will become the main focus of interest.

This passage (whose length may be justified initially by the fact that it corresponds to a whole 'sleepless night' in the source-material) is one of the finest not only in this play, but in the whole of Corneille's work; and apart from its formal qualities, its interest is twofold. First, it is a monologue in appearance only, being in reality a kind of dialogue between the two sides of the imperial personality – the would-be Auguste, and the has-been Octave. Secondly, it poses all the possibilities of physical violence which are latent throughout the play, as, in despairing irresolution, the emperor considers in turn abdication, surrender to assassination, destruction of the conspirators, suicide alone, and suicide combined with punishment of the traitors. This 'rigoureux combat d'un cœur irrésolu' (v. 1188) torn between duty to Rome, vengeance and the call of absolute power, is one of the great moments of moral drama. It remains unresolved, however:

Ou laissez-moi périr, ou laissez-moi régner.   (v. 1192)

– and the reason why it *must* remain unresolved at this stage is shown very subtly by Corneille in the manner in which the emperor designates himself only as *Octave* or as a *prince* (*princeps*) *malheureux*. What this brilliant speech makes clear, in short, is that he has not yet achieved the *venerable* personality implied by the name *Auguste*. He cannot in fact do so until he has experienced to the full the inadequacy of the satisfactions to be derived from an existence based on the power-motives of politics; and it is mainly with this in mind (as well as following the sources) that Corneille has made of Scene 3 the point in the play where the empress Livie intervenes to suggest that to pardon Cinna would be a wise move politically and a means of enhancing the imperial image (*renommée*, v. 1214); whereas the choice of abdication or death would be acts of despair rather than *générosité* (v. 1240), an abdication, in fact, of self-respect. Psychologically, therefore, the ground is being prepared for the act of clemency; but the time is not yet ripe because the emperor's moral confusion cannot be clarified without further revelations about the conspirators. The remainder of Act IV is thus directed to an analysis of the next stages in the breakdown of the conspiracy, beginning in Scene 4 with another evocation of the hopes and fears of Emilie, followed by the reappearance of Maxime, whose reported suicide is now revealed as trickery, and who, after trying unsuccessfully to persuade Emilie to flee with him, is left at the end of the act facing her accusations of treachery and overcome by futile remorse. Maxime is thus stripped of all dignity, and sees no hope of redemption save in killing the freedman whose counsels are blamed as the source of his own infamy. Murder appears once more, therefore, as a form of potential violence in the play; and the act ends, again, on a note of questioning – this time as to how far Maxime's remorse will take him.

With this display of Maxime's degradation the conspiracy, considered as a concerted enterprise, is at an end; and its members can only function for the time being as individuals, in their situations of danger or humiliation. The convergent movement of the action is now almost complete, and Corneille has contrived to reserve for the final act the confrontation of the emperor and the three conspirators in turn, which will produce over three scenes the ultimate climax of decision, and the denouement.

The first of these encounters is the celebrated scene (corresponding to a 'lecture' which, according to the sources, lasted more than two hours) in which the emperor reveals to the squirming Cinna his full knowledge of the young man's guilt. The latter's humiliation is so complete that his self-respect can, it seems, no longer be salvaged in life, but only in the prospect of death, provided that he can go to it unrepentant, claiming personal responsibility for the conspiracy and justifying it by his descent from Pompey. This clarifies the mind of the emperor as to the justice of executing Cinna, since, where there is no repentance, pardon is impossible. Ostensibly, therefore, Cinna is condemned not only to punishment, but to choosing the means. Yet, in accepting what he believes to be the prospect of death, Cinna claims that this will be essentially a *political* act on the part of the emperor.

But no sooner is this point reached when, in Scene 2, Emilie arrives to claim her share of responsibility. In doing so (with good motives), she destroys Cinna's previous claim to the dignity of sole responsibility; and she also affirms, like Cinna, that her death will be a political act, to ensure the safety of the emperor. Then follows a curious competition between the couple, as each claims responsibility in an attempt to salvage honour – a competition which can only be resolved when Emilie relents to the point of affirming that the conspiracy has been a joint enterprise for which they should be punished jointly as a couple. So, the scene ends with the emperor agreeing to satisfy them with an exemplary punishment; and *ostensibly*, death is again in the air, with this recognition of Emilie's guilt.

There can now only follow the reappearance of Maxime before the emperor who still believes him to have betrayed the others through loyalty, and who has already decided to pardon him for his spurious repentance. But in this final scene the truth is fully revealed as Maxime's humiliation drives him to repudiate the repentance which he has previously feigned, and affirm his willingness to die in the presence of the others, provided that Euphorbe is similarly punished for his degrading counsels.

Now the imperial cup of bitterness is full indeed; and so Corneille reaches a brilliantly paradoxical climax in which the declared political guilt of the conspirators removes all obstacles to political punishment by violence, but in which, against the run of superficial political logic, the emperor decides instead to offer them the hand of friendship, thus initiating through self-mastery a competition in *générosité*, at least in appearance.

> Je suis maître de moi comme de l'univers;
> Je le suis, je veux l'être. O siècles, ô mémoire,
> Conservez à jamais ma dernière victoire!
> Je triomphe aujourd'hui du plus juste courroux
> De qui le souvenir puisse aller jusqu'à vous.
>
> (vv. 1696–1700)

This, then, is the moment of the imperial 'apotheosis', in appearance one of emotional impulse rather than reason, as the conspirators accept the new benefits to be conferred on them – marriage for Cinna and Emilie, the consulate for Cinna, a restoration of the dignities of Maxime and a pardon for Euphorbe. So, the *submission* of the conspirators can now follow, the spirit of which is summed up by Emilie as one of *enlightenment*.

> Et je me rends, seigneur, à ces hautes bontés;
> Je recouvre la vue auprès de leurs clartés:
> Je connais mon forfait, qui me semblait justice;
> Et, ce que n'avait pu la terreur du supplice,
> Je sens naître en mon âme un repentir puissant,
> Et mon cœur en secret me dit qu'il y consent.
> Le ciel a résolu votre grandeur suprême;
> Et pour preuve, seigneur, je n'en veux que moi-même:

J'ose avec vanité me donner cet éclat,
Puisqu'il change mon cœur, qu'il veut changer l'Etat.
Ma haine va mourir, que j'ai crue immortelle;
Elle est morte, et ce cœur devient sujet fidèle.

(vv. 1715–26)

With this 'conversion' of Emilie and her companions, the State
is also changed, and – as Livie puts it in her last prophetic
speech – Rome at last surrenders fully to the man who has found
the true mastery – 'l'art d'être maître des cœurs' (v. 1764). So, in
the last speech of the play, it is truly *Auguste* whose voice is
heard, and who can legitimately designate himself by that name.

So concludes, in an atmosphere of *le merveilleux*, a work
which, despite a nominally happy ending, has plumbed the
depths of human anguish and frustration to arouse, without the
shedding of a single drop of blood, all the tragic emotions
associated with murder, assassination, suicide, surrender to
violence, and proscription – undeniably a *tour de force* in its
own category of dramatic art. But *Cinna* is not just a technical
masterpiece: it is a great play in that it can be appreciated at a
number of levels, and that its themes offer a perennial challenge
to criticism.

The Themes

The first and obvious level of thematic interest is *political*. Even
more, perhaps, than *Horace*, *Cinna* is concerned with the
emergence of a 'new order' within the whole history of Rome.
But since the primitive phase of the early monarchy, Rome has
rejected kings and lived through a long period of republican
liberty which, nevertheless, has degenerated into licence,
anarchy, brutality and, indeed, the *parricide* of civil war. From
this chaos, Octavian has emerged as the dominant political
figure, the victorious exponent of force and *de facto* 'monarch',
although his Principate is not recognized as a monarchy

because of the almost hereditary aversion of the Romans to the name of king. It is, moreover, constantly threatened by Octavian's defeated opponents or their descendants. The political problem running through the play is, therefore, whether the Romans can be induced to accept voluntarily not so much the fact as the *principle* or idea of absolute monarchy, which has become the only practical alternative to anarchy. This problem obviously *can* be related to the France of Corneille's time, though how far it *should* be so related remains debatable. In short, there are strong psychological resistances (amounting, indeed, almost to religious resistances) to be overcome before anyone can 'changer l'Etat' (v. 1724); and since the original monarchy is deemed to have broken down through the immoral abuse of power, the key to the acceptable reconstitution of an absolute authority must lie theoretically in the acceptance and practice of a new morality by Octavian, an advance to a new sense of moral responsibility which may win the 'hearts' of the people.

In the 'real' history of Rome (or at least the version of Cassius Dio), this process covers many years. But Corneille has here foreshortened the perspective of history in order to concentrate into one episode the essence of a long evolution, the direction of which is indicated by the gradual replacement by the *Princeps* of the 'Octavian' personality with the 'Augustus' personality, in accordance with the name conferred on him in 27 B.C. It is interesting to note, incidentally (in the light of *Horace*), that Octavian originally wished to assume the name Romulus, as a second 'father' of the city; and that in settling for 'Augustus', he was accepting a name with quite different moral associations and a quasi-religious connotation. This is one of the reasons why, in dramatizing the change from 'Octavian' to 'Augustus', Corneille is committed to a moral as well as a political theme.

If Cassius Dio offers the starting-point for the political play, the *moral* themes are derived largely (though not exclusively) from the Stoic concepts expressed in Seneca's *De Clementia*, but in passages other than the anecdote which provided the original subject. Leaving aside the possibility of 'opting out' by abdication or suicide, which is ruled out by history, examination of Corneille's text suggests that the 'moral ascension' of the emperor to the point at which he can refrain from inflicting physical punishment covers three main stages which are, in fact, clearly differentiated by Seneca. These are: *pity* (*misericordia*), *pardon* (*venia*), and true mercy or *clemency* (*clementia*). To understand Corneille's play, it is *essential* to realize that these terms are *not* synonymous.

According to the Senecan scheme, pity is, strictly speaking, a *weakness* of the mind, a sorrow brought about by the sight of the distress of others; and even a 'good' action occasioned by it cannot really be said to be motivated in the highest way, in a mind which is in complete control of itself. It cannot, in fact, emanate from a truly *free* will.

Pardon, says Seneca, is the remission of a *deserved* punishment, implying the omission of something that *ought* to be done; and morally speaking, it must remain a questionable act because of a flaw in the motivation. The reasons for pardoning would seem to be political rather than moral; and so such a gesture is to be conceived, again, as a reaction to circumstances rather than the 'free' act of the self-possessed mind.

This does not mean, however, that the wise man's acts need be outwardly very different from those of pity or pardon; it means simply that the motivation should be of a higher order. And it is in this sense that *clemency* is more 'complete and creditable' than pardon, because it rises above the letter of the law to the plane of genuine moral freedom: 'Mercy has freedom in decision' (*Clementia liberum arbitrium habet*).

There is thus something almost God-like about the genuine act of mercy; and this difference of intrinsic values is shown clearly in Corneille's play. For example, when, in response to Cinna's hypocritical arguments in Act II Scene 1, the emperor decides not to abdicate, it is explicitly out of *pity* for the possible plight of the Roman people without him.

> N'en délibérons plus, cette *pitié* l'emporte.
> Mon repos m'est bien cher, mais Rome est la plus forte;
> Et quelque grand malheur qui m'en puisse arriver,
> Je consens à me perdre afin de la sauver.   (vv. 621–4)

This action is apparently good, but is actually weak in that it represents an acquiescence rather than a free choice.

Similarly, in Act IV Scene 1, when Euphorbe's distorted account gives him to understand that Maxime is repentant, the emperor responds with an offer of *pardon*.

> Qu'Eraste en même temps aille dire à Maxime
> Qu'il vienne recevoir le *pardon* de son crime.
>
> > (vv. 1101–2)

But this pardon (which in any case remains inoperative because of Maxime's feigned suicide) is not the act of magnanimity that it might seem: it is merely an automatic response at the level of expediency, part of the political routine of *Octavian*. Thus the emperor is doing what he ought not to do, from a strict moral standpoint.

Significantly, it is Livie who, in Act IV Scene 3, while counselling 'pardon' for the conspirators as a politically useful act, manages at the same time to plant in her husband's mind the seed of the idea of *clemency*, with the aim of transforming him into a *vrai monarque*. Both terms occur in these ambiguous (or confused) 'conseils d'une femme'.

> Après avoir en vain puni leur insolence,
> Essayez sur Cinna ce que peut la *clémence*,
> Faites son châtiment de sa confusion;
> Cherchez le plus utile en cette occasion;
> Sa peine peut aigrir une ville animée,
> Son *pardon* peut servir à votre renommée (vv. 1209–14)

It will be noted that in the event Cinna does not escape punishment altogether, but that physical destruction is replaced by a moral humiliation which, while it lasts, is more 'tragic' than death, but which nevertheless leaves open a possibility of redemption. It is precisely this creative or redemptive potential which – again according to Seneca – distinguishes from mere pardon the 'free' act of clemency; and which makes it possible for the emperor to be not only 'maître de l'univers' and 'maître de soi' but also 'maître des cœurs', thus fulfilling the conditions necessary for the reconstitution and acceptance of a form of absolute monarchy.

In so far as the moral themes are exemplified by the emperor, there seems little doubt that the rationale of the play is derived from Seneca, whose discursive essay has been transformed into a history of enlightenment. It is thus entirely in keeping with the Senecan scheme that whereas the emperor's readiness to pity or to pardon is displayed in situations where the whole truth is not known, the final act of clemency follows a total revelation of the circumstances of the conspiracy, when there is theoretically complete 'freedom' for the exercise of the imperial will. But lest it be thought that Corneille is offering no more than an illustration of moral theory, it must be borne in mind that the enlightenment of Auguste is worked out in highly dramatic terms, and that his 'last victory' is nourished by the moral conflicts of each of the conspirators individually. For each of them manages to salvage a possibility of moral dignity from a situation of error, humiliation and defeat, either by the act of confession or in attaching moral value to the death which they believe they are facing. And it is a fine demonstration of Corneille's skill that the possibility of physical punishment remains open until almost the very end. The emperor may have decided to renounce such punishment before his interview with Cinna, but he still has to endure a series of temptations before he can be sure of the strength to forgive. These temptations form the substance of Act V, and they show again why it is only in the last line that he can truly and 'objectively' call himself 'Auguste' and proclaim his imperial *will*:

> Auguste a tout appris et *veut* tout oublier.
>
> (v. 1780)

Considered in terms of its political and moral themes, *Cinna* is an exceptionally fine adaptation of ancient source-material; and Auguste himself can be regarded as one of the more sympathetic of the so-called 'Cornelian heroes'. There is, however, more to the play than a political study or a set of moral exercises in the Stoic manner; and its interest today lies less, perhaps, in the philosophy than in the psychology, and above all, the subtle irony which can be found in it. For even if it is accepted at face-value as illustrating the creation of a new political and moral order through the conflict and suffering of individuals, in this case stopped short of actual violence, it is still possible to argue indefinitely as to the precise proportions of political and moral motivation in the action of Auguste, and the precise degree of irony which enters into the work of a playwright whose preoccupation with 'noble' subjects is some-times taken to imply that he never thought ironically about life.

The problems arise because while the 'new state' requires ostensibly a 'new man', the man we see at the end is still the same man, in certain respects. 'Maître de l'univers', 'maître de moi', 'maître des cœurs' – the operative word is still *maître*, and the psychology is still one of combat:

> Commençons un *combat* qui montre par l'issue
> Qui l'aura mieux de nous ou donnée ou reçue.
>
> (vv. 1705–6)

In other words, the will to dominate is still as much in 'Auguste' as in 'Octave', and it is perhaps the means that have changed rather than the man. But if this is so, it can be claimed that what Corneille has dramatized is not so much the regeneration of a *personality* as the successful adaptation to, and imposition of, a new *persona* or public image – i.e. the 'public relations exercise' which is in fact required by the political situation in Rome.

Be that as it may, it is a fact that 'Auguste' finally dominates those whom he has never wholly dominated as 'Octave'; and the crowning paradox of the play would seem to be that whereas *physically* the projected assassination fails because, being conditioned by the past, it is directed against 'Octave', yet *morally* 'Octave' *is* liquidated in circumstances which could be taken to imply that the successful 'assassin' is – Auguste! It is, therefore, not surprising that in all the key descriptions of him, the constant term should be *maître*.

5

Polyeucte

This play, produced in 1643, is commonly regarded as the peak of Corneille's achievement, partly because of its formal and stylistic qualities, but mainly because of the breadth and depth of its content. To begin with, it is a continuation and culmination of his 'Roman' subjects, in that it depicts through the experiences of individuals the impact of Christianity upon the Roman world. Secondly, by treating religious commitment in the extreme form that leads to martyrdom, it adds to the study of political and moral conflicts a spiritual dimension which promises an even greater degree of psychological interest; and thirdly, it includes an unusually poignant love-story.

The Subject

The story of the martyrdom of Polyeucte is retailed by the tenth-century hagiographer Metaphrastes, but the source quoted by Corneille is a version in the sixteenth-century *Vitae Sanctorum* of Surius and Mosander. This brief account tells of Néarque and Polyeucte, young men of high standing living in the province of Armenia in the year 250, just after the emperor Decius decreed one of the most serious persecutions of the Christians. Of the two, only Néarque is represented as a baptized Christian; and it is his anxiety over the effects of the persecution on their friendship which is said to have elicited from Polyeucte a declaration of his own Christian sympathies and desire to die for the faith. The causes of this desire are a growing respect for the teaching and acts of

Christ, as related to him by Néarque, and a vision, experienced the previous night, of Christ clothing him in a luminous
robe and mounting him on a winged horse in order to follow
him.

Polyeucte is not in fact baptized; but on being told by
Néarque that baptism is not absolutely necessary for entry into
heaven, is suddenly seized with an impulse of *sainte ferveur*
which prompts him to spit upon and destroy the imperial edict,
and smash the pagan idols which are being borne to the altars
for worship. This act takes place before Polyeucte's father-in-
law Félix, who holds an imperial commission to direct the
persecution; and on being faced with a situation which threatens
his own position, both public and domestic, Félix naturally
tries to shake Polyeucte's resolve by persuasion, menaces,
violence and, finally, through the tears of his daughter Pauline,
the young man's wife. At last, seeing that all this is of no avail,
and that Polyeucte's intransigence is winning other converts,
Félix has his son-in-law beheaded; and so, baptized only by his
own blood, Polyeucte goes to the glory reserved for those who
give up their lives for love of God.

In this case, there is no other source-material of any importance, except a victory by the emperor Decius over the Persians,
which serves as background for certain 'inventions and embellishments' which Corneille felt obliged to add to this curious
story.

The Adaptation of the Subject

Corneille himself summarized the major changes and additions
as: a dream of Pauline foreshadowing obscurely her husband's
death; the character of Sévère, a Roman knight and rejected
suitor of Pauline, believed dead but very much alive as the
emperor's favourite; the actual baptism of Polyeucte; a
sacrifice to commemorate Decius's victory, which is a pretext
for the presence of Sévère; the elevation of Félix to provincial

governor; the death of Néarque; and the conversion of Félix and Pauline.

These modifications (to which might be added the representation of Polyeucte and Pauline as a *newly-married* couple) are more than mere 'embellishments', since without them there would be little drama worthy of the name, little psychological interest and little scope for serious themes, but only a naïve exercise in the field of *le merveilleux chrétien* – a spectacle far too arbitrary to interest the seventeenth century, let alone the twentieth.

It may be assumed, nevertheless, that Corneille would not have selected this particular martyr-story unless it already offered a reasonable basis for a human drama; and it does, in fact, contain at least five elements capable of serious exploitation. First, the hint of a progressive religious awakening before the sudden act of iconoclasm provides the starting-point for a private drama of a *moral* and *spiritual* nature; secondly, the official status of Félix must obviously create a *political* perspective of some kind; thirdly, the tears of Pauline indicate a *domestic* tragedy; fourthly, the few words concerning the pressures exerted by Félix provide for a series of dramatic episodes; and lastly, the conversion of unspecified persons opens up a *historical* perspective. Thus, the main 'dimensions' of the drama are already discernible in the source; but their relationship is sufficiently loose to allow scope for creation, and to necessitate extensive reshaping in order to produce a unified whole.

It is characteristic of Corneille that he should have begun by 'rationalizing' as well as expanding the religious material. In the source, Polyeucte's experience has five main phases: namely, (i) the teaching of Néarque; (ii) the vision; (iii) the *impulsive* act of iconoclasm; (iv) the refusal to recant, producing other conversions; and (v) the actual martyrdom. In Corneille's version everything suggestive of superstition or totally irrational enthusiasm is toned down, and the process covers eight main phases.

(i) The teaching and influence of Néarque are integrated with the early action, thus allowing serious discussion of *doctrine*.

(ii) The *baptism* of Polyeucte is introduced as a more acceptable explanation of religious exaltation than the somewhat grotesque 'vision'; though a 'pagan' alternative appears in Pauline's dream, for atmospheric and emotional purposes.

(iii) The resulting act of *iconoclasm*, shared by Néarque, is reasoned and more deliberate, and its dramatic significance is thus heightened.

(iv) The *martyrdom* of Néarque is logical in itself, and dramatically useful.

(v) An episode of *prayer* is introduced (Act IV Scene 2), bringing enlightenment, exaltation, and rejection of the world through grace.

(vi) The *martyrdom* of Polyeucte takes place.

(vii) The *conversion*, not of unspecified persons, but of Pauline and Félix, takes place more logically *after* the martyrdom.

(viii) An indication of *tolerance* to come is given by Sévère, as the representative of the secular power nearest to the emperor.

In Corneille's hands, the subject clearly becomes less 'primitive'; but, although there are concessions to seventeenth-century theology and orthodoxy in these changes, they make for better dramatic effect, and confer on the religious subject greater dignity and integrity. They also make possible a more thorough and subtle analysis of religious experience, and a very serious treatment of intrinsic values, theology, and historical import. Furthermore, they strengthen the religious motivation at every step, allow for more conflicts and 'reversals', and intensify the challenge to the pagan establishment, thus leading to a more impressive and uncompromising confrontation at the end. But to get full value from these developments of the religious aspects, Corneille must obviously strengthen the secular side of the story as well; and it is in this that much of the merit and interest of the completed work lies.

In the original account the forces opposing Polyeucte are represented by Félix and Pauline; but the initiative is with the former, and the intervention of Pauline appears as little more than a last resort. Corneille, however, has seen that religious influences on one partner in a marriage could produce strong drama and profound tragedy, especially when there are other complications. He has chosen, therefore, to devote much of his creative effort to this element, which is barely adumbrated in the source; and consequently Pauline is given the biggest role of all. She appears in seventeen scenes and in every act, the reason being that she has a multiple function: namely, to play a more active part in hindering Polyeucte's progress to martyrdom; to undergo religious enlightenment herself; to create a 'triangle' as part of the love theme; and, in general, to serve as a permanent focus of *pathos* in the play. In developing this shadowy figure, Corneille has produced the most feminine and sympathetic of all his women characters, and the quality of the tragic emotion generated by her presence is one of the play's great merits.

Félix (whose importance has almost always been underrated) is another impressive piece of characterization, since Corneille, with his usual flair for what is significant in his sources, has realized that the less firm the persecutor, the more interesting the martyrdom can be made. Thus, the key to Félix, as developed by the dramatist, is a discrepancy between his function and his character; and from a few reported acts, Corneille has deduced and built up a character who can obviously not be wholly sympathetic, but who rings true, as a weak man confronting an appalling dilemma and intractable threat to his public and private life; and who is saddled, moreover, with a burden of responsibility which cannot be discharged 'by the book'. By making him provincial governor, Corneille not only increases his political and administrative responsibility, but creates an inconsistency within it. His general duty is to maintain 'law and order', but he must also enforce a particular policy of persecution which militates against this, as the challenge of his son-in-law shows only too well.

Between them, daughter and father provide substantial elements of domestic and political tragedy; but their personal tragedies might remain separate if it were not for Corneille's invention of Sévère, whose primary functions are to stimulate and unify the secular side of the drama. For Sévère comes into the play both as the emperor's favourite (and hence a political force acting on Félix), and as a private individual – the lover previously rejected by Pauline because of his lack of fortune, but only in obedience to Félix. And Félix now believes, understandably but mistakenly, that Sévère wants to discredit him with Decius, and will do so at any sign of neglect of duty.

Thus, within the public conflict between Christianity and the established order, and contributing to it, Corneille has created a group of characters held together in a whole system of private conflicts and dilemmas. Polyeucte is torn between two forms of the good: a transcendent love of God, and love of his newly-married wife. Pauline is divided between loyalty to her father and loyalty to a husband whom she does not understand, with the added complication of lingering regret for a love that she would have chosen had she been a free agent. Sévère is torn between honour and the temptation to profit from the extraordinary situation by trying to win back the love of Pauline. And Félix, always vacillating, is pulled apart by genuine affection for Polyeucte, love of his daughter, fear of the emperor, mistrust of Sévère, political ambition, and some genuine concern for justice and the pagan establishment. This is a situation in which no character can move without affecting the others, and in which all contribute something to the circumstances leading to the death of Polyeucte. So, the force and attraction of religious inspiration is complemented by the energy generated in this emotional tangle; and an unusual event is prepared, in the typical Cornelian manner, by a convergence of motives and circumstances.

The Dramatic Mechanism

Before examining this, a few additional points must be made concerning the importance of the characters. First, in so far as the play symbolizes the Christian take-over of the Roman empire, it naturally shows a bi-polarity similar to that of *Cinna*, with the characters orientated to the old or the new. Reduced to its simplest terms, this initial polarization can be schematized as follows:

Les Dieux

    ←Sévère←Félix←Pauline→Polyeucte→Néarque→DIEU

Décie

But the processes of conversion within the play will end by changing or strengthening the orientation of most of the characters towards the Christian God, leaving Sévère uncommitted but sympathetic, and thus in a position to urge upon the emperor a change of policy towards tolerance.

The relationship between the characters is of course complicated by private considerations, but it is clear that the central figure in this 'chain' is Pauline, caught in the conflict of father and husband, and still trying to stifle her feelings for Sévère. This explains why so much of the pathos is concentrated around her; why she has the biggest role; and why she can be said to hold the play together.

Flanking her are Polyeucte and Félix whose roles, it is interesting to note, are almost evenly matched, quantitatively as well as functionally. Further out from the centre of conflict, though nearer in some ways to the 'poles', are Sévère and Néarque; and although Néarque disappears after a time, leaving more scope for the development of Sévère, the latter's role remains to some extent peripheral, and is not in fact a very big one. This point is important because Sévère has often been regarded, notably during the incredulous eighteenth century, as the real hero of the play, by reason of his character as an *honnête homme*, his misfortune in love and his advocacy of religious tolerance. He is not, however, a *dramatic* hero, because until almost the end of the play, it is his *presence* which matters, rather than his *actions*. He is indispensable because of what the others, especially Félix, *think* he may do; and must therefore be regarded as a sort of 'catalyst' for the action, rather than as a genuine protagonist. In this respect, his function resembles that of Néarque, who can be most simply described as the pacemaker for Polyeucte, at least initially.

But if Pauline's role is largely a pathetic one, and that of Sévère somewhat limited and peripheral, this means that a major part in the mechanism *must* be reserved for Félix, and it is precisely *because* of his personal mediocrity that his contribution is so interesting. However much, and for whatever reason, Polyeucte may desire martyrdom, he cannot achieve it by himself. It takes at least two people to produce a martyrdom, just as much as a murder, because somebody has to give the order for it to happen; and when the somebody is as vacillating as the Félix created by Corneille, and the would-be martyr is his daughter's husband, the giving of the order itself becomes, paradoxically, a quasi-heroic act, in the sense that it takes the unhappy governor beyond the normal range of his behaviour. So, whatever additional refinements and complications are introduced, the exaltation of Polyeucte *must* be matched, sooner or later, by the exasperation of Félix, motivated by *fear*; and the play is structured very much with this in view, just as *Horace* is constructed to produce plausibility for the murder of Camille.

It begins with a relatively dynamic exposition-act, which highlights at once the conflict between religious imperatives and the legitimate claims of marital love. In Scene 1 Polyeucte, who has been brought by Néarque to the point of receiving baptism in secret, expresses a wish to defer it because of Pauline's dream of catastrophe; and it requires a most uncompromising statement of principle by Néarque to get the better of Polyeucte's tender solicitude for the wife he has just married after a long courtship. In Scene 2 he departs for his secret rendezvous despite Pauline's protests, leaving her, in Scene 3, complaining to her confidante Stratonice of the casual behaviour of husbands after marriage, and recalling the love of Sévère, now believed killed in battle after her enforced rejection of him. Sévère is still obviously her ideal, and she admits that her feelings for Polyeucte are based on duty rather than inclination, in a marriage accepted to advance her father's ambition.

> Je donnai par devoir à son affection
> Tout ce que l'autre avait par inclination.   (vv. 215–16)

But the immediate reason for this haunting memory of Sévère is her dream, in which a triumphant Sévère has appeared threatening vengeance on Polyeucte for marrying her. In this obscure vision, Polyeucte is dead; and it is significant that everybody – Sévère, the Christians, and especially Félix – is deemed to have contributed to his death. This will prove to be true, but the details are all distorted, since Pauline does not know the truth of Polyeucte's involvement with the Christians.

With this account of the dream, an atmosphere of foreboding is built up, which breaks into action as, in Scene 4, Félix announces in anguish that Sévère is alive and approaching the town, and that Pauline must see him in order to explain away her marriage and deflect his resentment. Once more, therefore, Pauline is to be the victim of her father's selfishness; and the act ends on the usual note of speculation, with important events pending on both sides of the play: i.e. Polyeucte's baptism and the meeting of Pauline and Sévère.

In Act II Corneille uses six scenes to continue the rhythm already established between the religious and the secular aspects of the subject. The first three concentrate on Pauline's drama of private sentiment and are constructed round her encounter with Sévère. Scene 1 leads up to it dramatically by introducing Sévère, with his hopes of a new and successful courtship based on the change in his fortunes, and despair as he learns of her recent marriage. Scene 2 is the encounter itself, in which the former lovers play out their inevitable drama of renunciation in the characteristically 'Cornelian' atmosphere of duty, personal *gloire*, mutual esteem and *générosité*, which, nevertheless, does not conceal the underlying anguish of sensibility.

> SÉVÈRE: Adieu, trop vertueux objet et trop charmant.
> PAULINE: Adieu, trop malheureux et trop parfait amant.
>
> (vv. 571–2)

Nor does Pauline's great effort stifle the fear of a jealous and violent clash between the two men in her life; and it is this fear which provides the theme and atmosphere of Scene 3, leading to the second half of the act and renewed emphasis on Polyeucte. In Scene 4 he returns from his secret baptism to find Pauline still in distress; but assures her that they are both gentlemen and that (as he puts it in Scene 5)

> Nous ne nous combattrons que de civilité. (v. 636)

Meanwhile, Félix has announced the sacrifice which is, amongst other things, the pretext for Sévère's presence; and this provides for a strong conclusion to the act in Scene 6, where Polyeucte reveals to Néarque his intention to overthrow the altars in the temple. Apart from arousing curiosity and suspense, this scene illuminates the psychology of the potential martyr, and reveals his need for positive action rather than a mere understanding of abstract ideas. It is therefore the occasion of a further clarification of doctrine, especially that of the precedence of love of God over love of the creatures; and a demonstration of the enthusiasm of the convert in whom the initial effects of grace have not weakened.

> Je suis chrétien, Néarque, et le suis tout à fait;
> La foi que j'ai reçue aspire à son effet.
> Qui fuit croit lâchement et n'a qu'une foi morte.
>
> (vv. 667–9)

But it is also the occasion for an argument as to the relative value of acts, and whether it is better to *live* or to *die* for faith. Néarque, in fact, being less recently baptized, is inclined to the former course rather than the latter; and it is at this stage, in a 'competitive' situation, that Polyeucte takes over from Néarque the religious initiative and persuades his friend to join him in smashing the idols. The central act of iconoclasm becomes, therefore, a *joint* enterprise and not that of one individual – a point comparable with the situation in *Horace* where the six combatants refuse as a group to draw back from their fight; and equally revealing as to Corneille's psychological insight.

In accordance with convention, the image-breaking takes place off-stage between Acts II and III, and the resulting lull is filled by a soliloquy of Pauline which projects forward into Act III all the atmosphere of her anxiety, but also continues an ironic situation deriving from her dream, in that a catastrophic event *is* occurring in the temple, but not the one she fears – i.e. a clash between husband and lover. In Scene 2, however, the suspense breaks as the horrified Stratonice reports what has actually happened, thus preparing for a series of scenes indicating public scandal and the individual reactions of Pauline and Félix.

Scene 2 is extremely important for its revelation of a development in Pauline's attitude to her husband. Irrespective of his 'error' and new status as an enemy of the state and the gods, she still has a contractual obligation to love him:

Je l'aimai par devoir: ce devoir dure encore.   (v. 790)

But a new note is also heard:

Je chéris sa personne, et je hais son erreur.   (v. 800)

By this distinction between the man and the Christian, Pauline opens up a possibility of trying to preserve Polyeucte from punishment by her father by an emotional appeal to both men, at a purely personal level; but it also introduces a factor which will help to bring about Pauline's own enlightenment and conversion.

In Scene 3 Pauline's first opportunity for such an appeal is presented by her father's indignation, which is deflected provisionally against Néarque, since the latter poses no personal problem. But the plea for Polyeucte obtains only the predictable response that a crime which is both a political offence and sacrilege cannot be pardoned on a basis of personal privilege; and that Félix's own line of duty transcends private interests. Polyeucte's only hope lies in recanting; and Félix believes that the sight of Néarque's death will suffice to bring this about. He is wrong, as usual, since even apart from principles, the fact that Polyeucte has himself talked Néarque into martyrdom makes it almost impossible, psychologically, for him to draw back. Pauline, however, knows her husband well enough to appreciate the deliberate nature of his challenge to the existing order. So, in Scenes 4 and 5, brilliantly built up from the source-material, Félix is shown in a state of genuine moral anguish, and facing a political dilemma occasioned on the one hand by the presence of Sévère, and on the other by an angry populace threatening a riot to release Polyeucte, because of his descent from the kings of pre-Roman times.

The enforced witnessing of Néarque's death is the first obstacle overcome by Polyeucte in the second major phase of his journey to martyrdom; and the first failure by Félix to find a way out. Then between Acts III and IV, the latter again threatens Polyeucte vainly with death, thus preparing for an admirable climax, sustained virtually through two whole acts, and worked out through a series of paradoxes.

Act IV opens with the greatest threat of all to Polyeucte's determination: namely, the announcement of Pauline's impending arrival to plead with him. Against 'un si fort ennemi' (v. 1091) Polyeucte feels so much human weakness that he needs all the help he can conceive, divine or human; and in a curious passage (vv. 1087–1100) prays first to God, and then to the dead Néarque, as intercessor, for help to meet the challenge of Pauline's distress. Then he begs his guards to send for Sévère, presumably with the intention of bestowing Pauline upon him (though Corneille refrains, typically, from indicating precisely either the reason for, or the source of, this inspiration). In Scene 2, however, there is less doubt, for these splendid verses or *stances* are an extended prayer and meditation, expressing the soul's ascension and, through grace, the renunciation of the world, including Pauline.

> Je consens, ou plutôt j'aspire à ma ruine.
> Monde, pour moi tu n'as plus rien:
> Je porte en un cœur tout chrétien
> Une flamme toute divine;
> Et je ne regarde Pauline
> Que comme un obstacle à mon bien.   (vv. 1139–44)

This outpouring of religious feeling is the prelude to an encounter of husband and wife (Scene 3) which is one of the most moving episodes of Cornelian drama, as Pauline appeals successively to reason, to Polyeucte's sense of public duty and, finally, to his compassion. And, paradoxically, these *unsuccessful* appeals *succeed*, though in a manner which she cannot yet understand; for whereas Polyeucte's religion has hitherto been between himself and God, he is now moved to pray for her, that she too may receive the faith.

C'est peu d'aller au ciel, je vous y veux conduire.

(v. 1284)

But it is not for him, it is for God to touch the heart by grace; and although his approaching death may contribute to this, all that he can do as an act of *générosité* on the human plane is to direct her towards marriage with Sévère (Scene 4). Yet it is precisely this manifestation of *générosité*, which in other circumstances would be offensive to a wife's sensibility, that makes it impossible for her to take the way which he indicates. For in Scene 5 Sévère admits his failure to understand Polyeucte's gesture, and in doing so deepens its effect by forcing upon Pauline a sudden realization that love has a dimension beyond the grasp of mere *honnêteté*. Though still not a Christian, Pauline's *gloire* forbids her to compromise her own integrity by marrying Sévère, who will, as she recognizes, have contributed to Polyeucte's death by his presence, however innocently.

She therefore appeals to him to preserve his own integrity by interceding with Félix, in the correct belief that fear of Sévère is likely to be the strongest motive driving her father to execute her husband; and the last scene of the act shows Sévère rising a second time above his disappointment to do this, unaware that it will have the contrary effect to that intended.

So the ground is at last fully prepared for the last act, in which the emphasis must fall largely on the confrontation of Polyeucte and Félix.

In the interval between the acts, Sévère is deemed to have made his attempt to soften Félix, but the first scene reveals its futility, since the governor, obsessed with his own fears, is incapable of seeing in Sévère's action anything but a trick to ruin him with the emperor. Nevertheless, being still unable to nerve himself to give the decisive order, Félix sends for Polyeucte in a last attempt to induce him to abjure, or at least to play for time. In Scene 2 he offers hypocritically to protect the

Christians, and even asks to be instructed in the faith – anything
to gain time until the departure of Sévère. From Polyeucte, the
only response is defiance and mockery – until he sees Pauline
enter to make a last appeal to both of them, and to shed the
tears which are the only indication of her tragedy in the source-
material. Félix gives way and adds his own pleas to those of his
daughter; but, ironically, as Félix is moved at last to forget his
political habits and speak sincerely as a sensitive human being,
Polyeucte's own mind is finally closed by the conviction that
these appeals are *ruses de l'enfer*. And it is in these circumstances
that his final challenge and 'blasphemy' is uttered against the
established order.

> J'ai profané leur temple et brisé leurs autels;
> Je le ferais encor, si j'avais à le faire,
> Même aux yeux de Félix, même aux yeux de Sévère,
> Même aux yeux du sénat, aux yeux de l'empereur.
>
> (vv. 1670–73)

And so Félix, the reluctant persecutor, is at last driven by
exasperation to *consent* to the execution, this being the peak of
his own 'effort' which, at the crucial moment is one of anger and
fear – in other words a paroxysm of pure emotion rather than
the calculation which is the basis of his normal activity.

But no sooner has he acted than he is denounced, first by
Pauline, as a *père barbare*, as she proclaims her own conversion.
And after Pauline, it is the turn of Sévère, who threatens him
with the social and political *ruine* which has been the greatest of
his fears, and condemns him equally as a *père dénaturé* and a
malheureux politique. For Félix, this is the moment of truth –
and despair; and in this moment, with his world in ruins, he
announces his own conversion.

> De ma fureur, je passe au zèle de mon gendre. (v. 1772)

So, the death of Polyeucte reconciles daughter and father in a

new faith: a 'miracle', according to Sévère, who makes the
response appropriate to the *honnête homme*, namely, a defence
of the middle way of tolerance. But he also – final irony – urges
Félix to resume the powers and functions which he has been
ready to abandon.

But if this conclusion is a 'miracle' (and this is not denied by
Corneille), it leaves for consideration a number of questions,
concerning verisimilitude in particular, which cannot be exam-
ined apart from the themes of the play.

The Themes

Like all of Corneille's great plays, *Polyeucte* contains a number
of themes combined so intricately that it is difficult, and
perhaps improper, to separate them out entirely. They illustrate
the values by which people live, the clash between different
values, or the difficulty of reconciling personal ideals with
social pressures or the brute realities of history; and the study
of individual characters can obviously throw light on them.
Sévère, for example, who starts as a stock seventeenth-century
literary type of *soupirant* or 'sighing suitor', becomes in
Corneille's treatment a serious representative of *honnêteté*, by
his fundamental decency and tolerance. And in so far as he
stands between the extreme Christian principles of Polyeucte
and the absence of any clear ethical principle in Félix, it could
be argued that he is more important to the themes of the play
than to the action.

Even the unhappy Félix (whose very name constitutes one of
the ironies of the play) represents a genuine conflict of public
and private loyalties; and – even more important – by his
prévoyance (v. 1502) or constant tendency to 'take thought for
the morrow', he demonstrates an attitude diametrically
opposed to an aspect of Christian teaching. And Pauline, for
her part, illustrates amongst other things the classic theme of
conflict between the sentimental and the contractual aspects of

marriage. Themes such as these, which are partly secular in
character, can be deduced fairly easily from the text; but there
are specific religious themes which may be less clear nowadays
than they were when the play was written.

Although Corneille has quoted sources for the *subject* in the
writings of obscure hagiographers, he has not mentioned in his
prefatory remarks the general source of inspiration for anything
purporting to be a Christian work: namely, the Bible itself. The
play does, however, contain textual echoes of it which sum up
the most important theme of all: i.e. the nature of the Christian
vocation and the extent of its demands. They are heard in a
speech of Néarque in the first scene.

> Il ne faut rien aimer qu'après lui, qu'en lui-même,
> Négliger, pour lui plaire, et femme, et biens, et rang.
>
> (vv. 74–5)

and are repeated by Polyeucte in Act II Scene 6, when it is his
turn to encourage Néarque.

> Il faut (je me souviens encor de vos paroles)
> Négliger, pour lui plaire, et femme et biens, et rang.
>
> (vv. 686–7)

By a stroke of irony, they are also heard from Félix, but in the
form almost of a parody:

> Les Dieux et l'empereur sont plus que ma famille.
>
> (v. 930)

Later, in Act V Scene 2, when Félix offers hypocritically to
protect the Christians, Polyeucte replies:

> Non, non, persécutez,
> Et soyez l'instrument de nos félicités:
> Celle d'un vrai chrétien n'est que dans les souffrances;
> Les plus cruels tourments lui sont des récompenses.

Dieu, qui rend le centuple aux bonnes actions,
Pour comble donne encor les persécutions. (vv. 1533–8)

And when Polyeucte is resisting the pleas of Pauline, he refers
repeatedly to a wife who is an enemy, to be fought.

O présence, ô combat que surtout j'appréhende!
(v. 1082)

Et je ne regarde Pauline
Que comme un obstacle à mon bien.   vv. 1143–4)

Apportez-vous ici la haine ou l'amitié,
Comme mon ennemie, ou ma chère moitié?
(vv. 1165–6)

The ideas in these speeches derive ultimately from a few biblical
texts mostly concentrated in one or two well-known passages of
St Matthew or St Mark: e.g. (Authorized Version) Matthew X,
34–36, 39

Think not that I am come to send peace on earth: I came
not to send peace but a sword.

For I am come to set a man at variance against his father,
and the daughter against her mother. . . .
And a man's foes shall be they of his own household.

He that findeth his life shall lose it: and he that loseth his
life for my sake shall find it.

and Mark X, 29–31 (Cf. Matthew XIX, 29–30).

And Jesus answered and said . . . There is no man that hath
left house, or brethren, or sisters, or father, or mother, or
wife, or children, or lands, for my sake and the gospel's,

But he shall receive an hundredfold now in this time...
with persecutions; and in the world to come eternal life.

But many that are first shall be last; and the last first.

On the religious side, these are the teachings which reveal what
Polyeucte is really *about*: i.e. Christianity as a challenging and
possibly disruptive force; as a *paradoxical* experience, from the
standpoint of 'reason'; and as a possible source of a type of
domestic tragedy (which, it is interesting to note, would
presumably have been approved by Aristotle!).

Although there are things in the play which may seem in-
comprehensible and even repugnant, their origin and justification is not in Surius or Metaphrastes but at the fountain-head
of Christian teaching. One example is the thing which is apt to
provoke most resistance of all: namely, that the wretched
Félix is converted, while the estimable Sévère is not. The short
answer to this problem might well be that Félix is indeed one of
the last who shall be first; but there are, of course, longer
answers, one of which involves the concept of divine grace,
which provides another basic theme of the work.

When Corneille wrote it, this concept was becoming the
subject of great controversy in France, particularly between the
Jansenists and the Jesuits, the first of whom stressed its
arbitrary nature, in contrast to the Jesuits, whose doctrines
made more allowance for freewill and progressive human effort
as part of the processes of salvation. And while it is agreed that
the religious aspect of *Polyeucte* can be interpreted as an
illustration of the working of grace, there has been perennial
argument as to whether Corneille was committed to one or
other of the contemporary views of the subject. The most
sensible answer seems to be that he was not; and that writing
as a dramatist and not as a theologian, he represented grace as
mysterious, but necessarily variable in operation, in order to
meet the needs of all sorts and conditions of men. Hence, if the

religious element in *Polyeucte* is taken at face-value, it is quite reasonable that the converted characters should show different degrees of commitment, and that the processes of conversion should not always be the same. In the play, two persons are martyred, but not by identical processes; and similarly, the operation of grace differs as between Polyeucte, Pauline and Félix, if only because they are people of completely different temperament, and must arrive at communion with God through individual experiences and combinations of motives. Polyeucte is essentially practical and energetic, and religion offers him, apart from anything else, an outlet for his energy; Pauline moves towards God through a comparative experience of human love; and Félix makes the leap of faith mainly from despair and the failure of the worldly calculations which he has followed hitherto, but which he believes, at the crucial moment, to have brought him to ruin. In this connection it is essential to remember Sévère's threat to him in Act V Scene 6:

> Et par votre *ruine* il (Sévère) vous fera juger
> Que qui peut bien vous perdre eût pu vous protéger.
>
> (vv. 1757–8)

and compare this with Polyeucte's prayer in Act IV Scene 2:

> Je consens, ou plutôt j'aspire à ma *ruine*.
> Monde, pour moi tu n'as plus rien.   (vv. 1139–40)

This is one of the details that confirm the complementary and convergent nature of the actions of the two men; for if Polyeucte's aspiration to martyrdom is necessary to God's ultimate purpose, then so is the 'collaboration' of Félix; and it does not matter that the worldly 'ruin' of the one should appear voluntary, and that of the other involuntary. Both contributions are necessary according to the transcendent 'logic' of grace, which may well be paradox in the sight of men.

From the religious standpoint, therefore, the conversion of Félix is comprehensible as one particular manifestation of grace, and also, perhaps, of divine mercy for a man whose suffering and responsibility have had to be disproportionate to his moral resources; but we need not on that account be content with the term 'miracle' which Corneille himself accepts in his *Examen* of the play. For one of his greatest achievements in *Polyeucte* is to have provided a plausible psychological basis even for such 'miracles', and thus to have breathed life into theological propositions.

Since Christianity is a religion of love, any work which purports to treat it seriously must have love as a leading theme; and this explains why Corneille, who had reservations about it as a subject for tragedy in general, had no inhibitions about it in this particular work. For at the heart of the play there is perhaps the most moving conflict conceivable; and an exploration of the problems posed by the Christian injunctions concerning love of God, love of neighbour, and love of self. And if 'wife' be included under the heading of 'neighbour', it becomes clear that from the Christian standpoint, Polyeucte's aspiration to martyrdom is above all an experience in the order of love, ending in complete spiritualization, though not without bitter struggles on the way.

To begin with, in his half-enlightened state, Polyeucte would certainly compromise out of carnal love for Pauline, seeing an apparent conflict between love of God and his earthly love; and there are moments when his preoccupation with Heaven could be -- and sometimes is -- interpreted as egoistic. But his final position is expressed straightforwardly enough:

> Je vous aime,
> Beaucoup moins que mon Dieu, mais bien plus que
> moi-même   (vv. 1279–80)

Taking the orthodox approach, it must be assumed that the

ultimate fulfilment of this *conjugal amour* will be in the here-after; in so far as Pauline does, in the course of the play (and through the operation of 'esteem' as well as grace) transfer her affection from Sévère to her husband.

There are, needless to say, possibilities of analysing their relationship in less orthodox ways; but these raise questions of a different order which are best treated with more general problems of appreciation posed by Corneille's works as a whole.

Interpretation and Appreciation

Even more than most classics, Corneille's masterpieces have suffered from stereotyped interpretations, with the result that today it is difficult to appreciate him without first examining, and to some extent discarding, certain critical prejudices which have too often distorted the significance of his work. The most important of these are concerned with 'heroism'.

The Traditional Idea of the Cornelian Hero

Even during the seventeenth century, and mainly because of over-simplified comparisons with the tragedies of Racine, so often regarded as no more than pessimistic and fatalistic representations of destructive passion, the idea established itself that Corneille presents human nature in its noblest, most positive and most energetic aspects. This opinion appears in a famous judgement of the moralist La Bruyère in his book, *Les Caractères* (1688), to the effect that Corneille depicts men as they ought to be, whereas Racine depicts them as they are. Like many neatly-turned generalizations, La Bruyère's formula is plausible enough to have imposed itself on subsequent generations, and its effects are still visible.

It suggests that Cornelian drama is essentially a heroic spectacle or *display*: an 'aristocratic' genre presenting socially elevated characters performing unusual actions beyond the capacity of ordinary mortals. Although these actions may be morally questionable or disastrous in their outcome, there is a standing implication that the characters themselves are in some sense exemplary, as personifications of human energy carried to the point of 'sublimity'; and that the proper response to them is one of awe, if not positive admiration. Consequently, the 'typical' Cornelian character is commonly conceived and described as superhuman or inhuman.

First impressions of figures like Horace or Polyeucte obviously lend some support to these interpretations, and it has been found relatively easy to rationalize and elaborate such impressions in historical or philosophical terms. So, the 'Cornelian hero' has been deemed to represent in a general and somewhat abstract way the essential human attributes of reason and freewill, applied to the limit in specific situations of conflict; and the plays are supposed to exemplify the evaluation of courses of action through reason, and subsequent commitment through sheer will-power – a process bringing to the character concerned a particular satisfaction which is associated with the word *gloire*. This rather elastic term covers everything from public reputation or honour to the private pride of achievement which comes from living up to one's highest values or most extreme aspirations; and the frequency with which the concept appears in the texts is one of the reasons why Corneille's theatre might seem to be an ingenious assembly of contrasting or conflicting *postures* rather than a reflection of real life.

To offset this impression of artifice, it is often claimed that Corneille is merely giving expression to forms of flamboyant individualism which actually existed in his day; or, alternatively, that he was drawing on well-worn traditions such as Stoicism or the medieval code of chivalry. Parallels have also been suggested between the behaviour of Cornelian characters and certain theories of the contemporary philosopher, Descartes, on the function of reason and will, expressed, notably, in the latter's *Traité des Passions* of 1649; but these must be treated with extreme caution for several reasons, including those of chronology, since the great plays appeared before the systematization of Descartes's ideas.

While opinions have differed as to the relative importance of possible sources of inspiration, the persistence of 'heroic' interpretations has led to some neglect of the totality of given plays and a tendency on the part of critics to concentrate attention upon specific characters who establish a dominance simply by following a line of conduct to the extreme limit. One consequence of this is that figures such as Horace, Auguste or Polyeucte have been seen more or less in isolation as variants of certain *preconceptions* about human nature, constructed *a priori*, as it were, and distinguishable from each other mainly by the values to which they are committed respectively. From this, it is not difficult to assume that Corneille's theatre is an intellectual exercise based on concepts rather than on people; and that he simply presents 'the patriot' or 'the martyr' as variants of a basic type. And critics have not shrunk from going further and asserting that in the final analysis his characterizations should not be judged as realistic exercises in individual psychology.

Given the stereotyped conception of the 'Cornelian hero', it is hardly surprising that his drama presents problems of appreciation at a time when anti-heroism is more fashionable anyway, and when the forms of expression cannot but seem stiff and archaic. Nevertheless, Corneille not only survives but has been gaining in esteem, for reasons which may be deduced to some extent from trends in recent criticism.

New Views of Corneille

An interesting indication of possible re-appraisals appears in an article published by M. Sartre in 1946, which, while accepting the traditional emphasis on the importance of the will in Corneille, expresses a radical opposition to La Bruyère's celebrated dictum about 'men as they ought to be' and maintains that by his analysis of the application of the will in specific and concrete situations, Corneille is actually nearer than is

Racine to the complexity of human reality. It is not difficult to see why the self-assertion and apparent voluntarism of Cornelian figures should appeal to an existentialist believing that a man in the process of creating himself is the most moving thing the theatre can show; and why the ostensible creation of 'new orders' in plays like *Cinna* or *Polyeucte* might be related in some degree with the existential choice. Anachronistic or not, this is at least a *possible* way of looking at Corneille; and it explains the emergence of an existentialist line of interpretation presenting the hero as a self-made man, and humanity in general as the source of values in the world.

This angle of approach is not, however, likely to satisfy everybody, and in other recent studies the plays have been explained in the opposite way, in that the choices made and adhered to are held to represent conformity to existing values and orders rather than the creation of new ones, and the heroic effort is regarded essentially as one of recognition and fulfilment.

These opposing points of view can be, and probably will be, argued indefinitely; but what they have in common is that they both encourage a belief that Corneille is above all a philosopher – playwright who cannot be fully appreciated below a certain level of intellectual analysis. This is a standing invitation to critics to produce *different* philosophical interpretations. These have duly appeared, with differing degrees of historical justification; and there is now a fairly wide choice of Corneilles on the market – Christian, Atheist, Stoic, Hegelian, Marxist and so on. There is, of course, no reason to condemn any of these approaches in so far as they help to illustrate the universality of this great playwright, and prove that he has something to say to every age; but they do have drawbacks, the most obvious of which is that no single 'philosophy' seems capable of providing a convincing explanation of the whole of Corneille's great and varied output. The most that can be hoped is that they may emphasize certain elements of consistency in particular series of plays, one of which is, precisely, that which runs from *Le Cid* to *Polyeucte*.

The Coherence of the Four Great Plays

It has been enthusiastically argued (e.g. by Charles Péguy) that *Polyeucte* is not only a peak of technical achievement, but a climax in a more profound sense. The line of such arguments is that having, with *Le Cid*, arrived at a fruitful formula for serious drama of moral crisis: i.e. the transcending of suffering by moral strength achieved in conflict, Corneille has gone on to apply the formula in the 'Roman' plays in such a way as to produce a vision of mankind's progressive enlightenment, achieved at a cost of individual suffering, but culminating in a genuine approach to God. On this view, there does seem to be a philosophy of history running through these great plays, which, if taken seriously, has some interesting implications. One of them is that Corneille lacks a genuine 'tragic sense'; or that the tragedy of the parts is transcended by the optimism of the whole. Another is that the levels of behaviour analysed in these successive works are gradually becoming less 'primitive'.

Now it can obviously be argued against this that behaviour in *Le Cid* or *Horace* is already highly sophisticated; nevertheless, progression of a sort does appear to take place: for example, in the absorption of lesser loyalties into larger loyalties, or the extension of the understanding of self-interest. Thus in *Le Cid* individual lovers surrender their immediate hopes to the claims of family honour; and in the end enhance their love by doing so (at least ostensibly). Similarly, in *Horace* whole families are sacrificed in a conflict of clan-loyalties from which, nevertheless, is born a more effective political organization. In *Cinna* – again ostensibly – the political establishment is itself transformed through the moral advance and enlightened self-interest of its leader; and in *Polyeucte* the struggle of individuals to attune their existence to religious values is again shown as re-activating and re-orientating the existing political society.

On the face of it, therefore, Corneille does seem to be moving consistently up a scale of values; and one of the criteria by which this can be measured is the use and moderation of physical violence. In *Le Cid*, private and public conflicts are resolved by the sword, and morality is subject to political expediency. The same is true of *Horace*, although here patriotism is elevated almost to the religious plane, and moral considerations are beginning to place restrictions upon the play of force (as is shown by the representative combat). But in *Cinna* crude violence is apparently superseded as a political instrument by the force of moral example, and the renunciation of bloodshed by Auguste might be viewed as the highest achievement of pagan ethics. In contrast to this, the reappearance of death and violence in *Polyeucte* may seem to be a retrogression; but this is not really the case, because the play is concerned with an urge not to *take* life, but to *surrender* life, and the unsuccessful attempts of other characters to prevent the would-be martyr from having his way. This is certainly in accordance with the Christian perspective; and to that extent the play could be seen as a 'conquest' over and beyond the horizon of *Cinna*. So, although the role of force may be only a crude measuring instrument, it does help to show why critics have claimed to see a logical progression in this series of plays, and taken it as evidence of a coherent vision of life and history in the mind of their author, at least at one period in his career.

Now if all this is accepted at face-value, it would indeed appear that these works are not only 'heroic' but also edifying in a sense which would justify the 'ought' in La Bruyère's formula, or allow them to be viewed as exercises in abnormal rather than normal psychology, in which the initiative and suffering of exceptional individuals stakes out the path of human enlightenment. But against this superficially attractive interpretation it cannot be said too often that what Corneille has really tried to do is not simply to display human grandeur, but to *explain* dramatic events by the provision of credible motivations and plausible backgrounds. It is for this reason that his plays *must* be seen in relation to his source-material, if his creative powers are to be appreciated.

The Credibility and Relevance of Corneille

One implication of the old 'heroic' interpretation is that Corneille's characters create or control their own destiny, so that his work is really the antithesis of fate-tragedy. This, however, is highly debatable, because they are not responsible for their initial situations, and because the decisive acts are not, in fact, brought about through the volition of single individuals. It is, therefore, much better to start from the proposition that Corneille is first and foremost a *play-maker*, and a recognition that whatever happens in his plays is determined in the first instance by the *conclusion* – the terminus which is laid down by history or legend. If tradition says that Chimène married her father's killer, or that Horace became at once a hero and a murderer, there must be reasons for these things. However unlikely Auguste's change of heart and policy may seem, there must be a credible combination of circumstances to account for it. And although martyrs are uncommon, they are not so uncommon as to lie wholly beyond the range of ordinary psychological explanation, in specific situations. In other words, Corneille works on the assumption (opposed to the views of many contemporaries) that what is 'true' must be 'probable'; and much of the fascination of his work lies in this manipulation of characters and situations in such a way as to produce the ostensibly improbable conclusion without sacrificing basic human truth.

Looked at in this way, all of his major plays are serious and viable attempts to explain what may not be satisfactorily explained by his sources; and the invention of events or characters is rigidly conditioned by this requirement. The result of this is that the characters – including the so-called 'heroes' – acquire their dramatic stature through their *reactions* as much as by their *actions*. Thus, the tragic status of Horace depends not only upon his own patriotic idealism, but on that of his fellow-combatants, not to mention his domestic situation and the emotional nagging of Camille; Auguste's gesture is a response to a whole series of challenges; Polyeucte's martyrdom requires the collaboration of Félix, the example of Néarque and the upsetting of his domestic situation by the presence of Sévère; and so on. So, whatever personal resources of reason and will may be involved, decisive action cannot take place without the stimuli – particularly the emotional stimuli – provided within the whole group. This does not mean, however, that all psychological interest is transferred to the group at the expense of the individuals; for such is the complexity of motivation that it is never absolutely certain which is the decisive motive at a crucial and explosive moment in these plays. Just as it is impossible to be really sure of the final attitude of Chimène, so Corneille carefully refrains from indicating explicitly whether Auguste acts as he does through political acumen, moral idealism, emulation or even sheer contempt for the conspirators. And while *Polyeucte* may be taken straightforwardly as a drama of divine grace and Christian idealism (composed, incidentally, with the greatest skill and integrity), it can also be seen as a remarkable domestic drama, a variant of the eternal triangle with martyrdom as the unusual way out. Polyeucte may represent something like the ultimate in religious commitment; but – rightly or wrongly – he can be, and has been, regarded also as a man contracting out of a disappointment brought about by the 'resurrection' of the noble Sévère; or as a husband establishing an ascendancy over his wife at the cost of his own life. Given such a degree of complexity, the most sensible conclusion to draw from it is that Corneille meant to show that no simple or single impulse can explain the events he has dramatized, and that many threads enter at all times into the tissue of life. There is nothing here that accords with the celebrated myth of the Cornelian hero, but much to confirm that Corneille was a shrewd observer of human realities. It may be that for purposes of the theatre he has selected and exaggerated; but his masterpieces are nevertheless psychologically sound, and by no means as remote from common experience as might be thought, even in the basic situations. *Le Cid* presents universal themes of love and conflict; *Horace* prompts the reflection that relatives *have* been mobilized in opposing military machines in the course of the twentieth century; martyrs *do* appear to reveal mankind to itself; and although Roman emperors are in short supply, the political, moral and personal problems confronting Auguste must be at least comprehensible to any man who has reached the summit of ambition and found that he can neither stand still nor cancel the past.

In short, the persistence of conflict – and achievement – in human affairs and the complexity of motivation remain, as they always have been, the final justifications for the best of Corneille's theatre.

Bibliography

Antoine Adam, *Histoire de la littérature française au XVIIe siècle*, Vols. I, II and IV, Domat, Paris, 1948–54

H. C. Lancaster, *A History of French Dramatic Literature in the Seventeenth Century*, Johns Hopkins, Baltimore, 1929–42

P. Bénichou, *Morales du grand siècle*, Gallimard, Paris, 1948

J. Rousset, *La littérature de l'âge baroque en France*, J. Corti, Paris, 1953

J. Schérer, *La Dramaturgie classique en France*, Nizet, Paris, 1950

R. Brasillach, *Pierre Corneille*, Arthème Fayard, Paris, 1938

O. Nadal, *Le Sentiment de l'amour dans l'œuvre de Pierre Corneille*, Gallimard, Paris, 1948

G. Lanson, *Corneille*, Hachette, Paris, 1898

L. Herland, *Corneille par lui-même*, Eds. du Seuil, Paris, 1954

P. J. Yarrow, *Corneille*, Macmillan, London, 1963

S. Doubrovsky, *Corneille et la dialectique du héros*, Gallimard, Paris, 1963

R. J. Nelson, *Corneille. His Heroes and their Worlds*, University of Pennsylvania Press, Philadelphia, 1963

J. Maurens, *La Tragédie sans tragique. Le néo-stoïcisme dans l'œuvre de Pierre Corneille*, Armand Colin, Paris, 1966

A. Stegmann, *L'Héroisme cornélien*, 2 Vols., Armand Colin, Paris, 1968

H. T. Barnwell, ed., *Corneille: Writings on the Theatre*, Blackwell, Oxford, 1965